Art in a Democracy

Vol 2

This volume is the second in a two-volume set; *see also*
Volume 1: The Appalachian History Plays, 1975–1989

Art in a Democracy

Selected Plays of Roadside Theater

Volume 2:
The Intercultural Plays, 1990–2020

Ben Fink, Series Editor

New Village Press • New York

Published in the United States by New Village Press
bookorders@newvillagepress.net
www.newvillagepress.org
New Village Press is a public-benefit, nonprofit publisher

Distributed by NYU Press

Paperback ISBN: 978-1-61332-194-2
Hardcover ISBN: 978-1-61332-195-9
EBook ISBN: 978-1-61332-196-6
EBook Institutional ISBN 978-1-61332-197-3

Publication Date: March 2023

First Edition

Library of Congress Control Number: 2022950529

Cover Design: Kevin Stone
Cover Photo: Ron Short and John O'Neal perform *RoadBug*, Whitesburg, Kentucky. Photo by Tim Cox.

Dedicated to you, Reader.
May you find something useful;
may you find something to build on.

The problem for the modern poet, as for every one else today, is how to find or form a genuine community, in which each has his valued place and can feel at home. The old pre-industrial community and culture are gone and cannot be brought back. Nor is it desirable that they should be. They were too unjust, too squalid, and too custom-bound. Virtues which were once nursed unconsciously by the forces of nature must now be recovered and fostered by a deliberate effort of the will and the intelligence. In the future, societies will not grow of themselves. They will either be made consciously or decay. A democracy in which each citizen is as fully conscious and capable of making a rational choice, as in the past has been possible only for the wealthier few, is the only kind of society which in the future is likely to survive for long.

—W. H. AUDEN, *THE OXFORD BOOK OF LIGHT VERSE*, 1939

Contents

Introduction to Volume 2

Roadside Theater's founders had three related questions on their minds when the company got started in 1975: Could a small group of community-trained musicians, storytellers, and writers in the coalfields of central Appalachia create a professional theater in a place with no history of the same? Could the form and content of such a theater be created from local sources? And finally: Could the ensuing dramas appeal to people anywhere?

By 1990, after creating new plays and successfully touring them across the United States, we found the answer to all three questions was, against the odds, an emphatic *Yes!* The plays' content was informed by stories, ballads, and oral histories collected firsthand and through archival research. The theater's distinctive style, telling stories interwoven with acting and music, was drawn from mountain preachers, singers, and traditional storytellers. Roadside performers batted lines back and forth, saying some phrases in unison, feeding off one another's rhythms, and telling the whole story together. There was always enough ambient light in the auditorium for the audience to see itself, and there was no conceit of a "fourth wall" separating the stage from the audience: Actors and audiences interacted naturally, in the same way that preachers and congregations participated in call-and-response. And as at church, people onstage and off lingered in fellowship long after the performance was over. At its best, a Roadside event was a form of secular communion.

The five plays included in volume 1, created during the company's first fifteen years, depict the history of people living in the central Appalachian mountains from the European incursion through the Vietnam War. At home, these plays drew an audience that matched the plays' poor and working-class characters—and the background of the plays' performers. But on tour in hundreds of communities across forty-five states, our audiences came mostly from the wealthiest 15 percent. This audience mismatch not only hindered Roadside's pursuit of democracy; it also subverted the meaning of the plays themselves. Roadside actors, playing off the audience as always, found themselves shortening or even deleting text that elite audiences did not like or understand. After one such performance, a performer confessed that despite the full exertion of her will, she could feel herself becoming Elly May Clampett, the stereotypical hillbilly of *The Beverly Hillbillies*.

In response to this challenge came the question that would guide Roadside's work for the following three decades: Who's in the house, who's left out, and how do we bring them in? The introduction to volume 1 describes some of Roadside's first steps in this direction, including our risky business decision in 1989 to perform only in communities that would contractually agree to build an audience that looked like their whole community. But we soon found ourselves facing a set of problems too big and ingrained for one small theater company to tackle alone.

•   •   •

In 1965, at the height of the civil rights movement, and ten years before Roadside was founded, Congress established the National Endowment for the Arts (NEA) and the National Endowment for the Humanities (NEH). Echoing the populist vision of the Federal Theatre Project, the new law's "Declaration of Findings and Purposes" asserted: "The arts and humanities belong to all people of the United States." As in the 1930s, the foundation was being laid for a flourishing of democratic art across the country. By 1980, the NEA had become the nation's largest single arts funder, commanding respect across the field for supporting artistic excellence in all its diverse forms. Private foundations began following the NEA's lead.

But just as J. Edgar Hoover and his associates helped to terminate the Federal Theatre Project in 1939, so did Ronald Reagan and his allies set out to destroy the NEA and NEH when they came to power in 1981. Never able to garner enough votes in Congress to abolish the endowments outright, they instead took up the strategy of death by a thousand cuts. These cuts would continue during Democratic and Republican administrations alike, part of a broader anti-community agenda that has defined public policy for the past forty years: privatizing public goods and public spaces, defunding community-led organizations, and otherwise creating a cultural and economic reality where there isn't enough to go around. We are all still living with the results: widening wealth and income gaps, soaring health care and housing and education costs, and a polarizing media environment that encourages us to see our neighbors as threats rather than as fellow citizens and allies. As resources declined and incarceration rates increased dramatically, politicians here in the mountains began selling prisons as a remedy for poverty, tying the economic survival of rural and majority-white Americans to the imprisonment of urban and majority-Black Americans. A perfect storm was brewing, less by chance than by design.

Small and grassroots-led organizations like Roadside, which relied on public support in lieu of donations from wealthy patrons, felt the immediate effects of these anti-democratic policies. We watched them closely, and formed alliances to fight back. In 1976, Roadside cofounded Alternate Regional Organization of Theaters South (Alternate ROOTS), a network of southern "people's theater" ensembles committed to justice. Alternate ROOTS had its birth at the Highlander Center, perched atop a mountain near New Market, Tennessee. Highlander had long carried the torch of populism in the South: During the 1930s labor movement, it was the southern training center for the newly formed Congress of Industrial Organizations (CIO), and during the 1960s civil rights movement, it birthed the Citizenship Schools and trained grassroots activists like Rosa

Parks. ROOTS attempted to follow in the same tradition; it eventually became a coalition of more than two hundred southern artists and organizations celebrating the cultural genius of southern communities and wrestling with the South's histories of injustice.

It was Highlander's director Myles Horton who first put Roadside in touch with John O'Neal, who had cofounded the Free Southern Theater in 1963 with several other members of the Student Nonviolent Coordinating Committee (SNCC) as part of their efforts to organize communities across the Deep South during the civil rights movement. As with Roadside, the work of the Free Southern Theater was inspired by local histories, songs, and stories, kept alive in the oral traditions of the Black Belt of Louisiana and Mississippi. Horton, who had a dry sense of humor, suggested O'Neal check out an upstart theater company over in Whitesburg, Kentucky—quipping that they, too, appeared to be nationalists. O'Neal picks up the story:

> I met Roadside's director, Dudley [Cocke], in 1977 in Florida at a ROOTS theater festival. Dudley said, "John, what did you think of our little play?" Now Myles had told me that Roadside was performing for poor and working-class white people in Southern Appalachia, and near Knoxville, Tennessee was where the KKK was founded. So I said, "From what I understand about what y'all are doing, you have a lot of potential Klansmen in your audience, and, frankly, I didn't see anything in your play that would make a potential Klansman less likely to be a Klansman than before he listened to your story." I had some experience working with white people, and I knew that this kind of aggressive, though polite, response had a tendency to push them up against the wall. And I liked to get them there and place needles in them and hold them like specimens to see what they would do. Dudley, he didn't miss a beat, said, "Hmmm, what do you think we ought to do about that, John?" Now I came there not planning on doing shit. I came to keep an eye on what the white people were doing. That's what started the work that we continue to do together, now going on 35 years. [O'Neal continued to work with Roadside until shortly before he passed away, in 2019.]

We first agreed to host each other's performances and workshops in our home communities. This exchange lasted more than a decade, offering a rare chance for people in both places to get to know one another. In 1981, O'Neal invited Roadside to take part in a traditional New Orleans second-line funeral to bury the Free Southern Theater—and witness the birth of Junebug Productions. The weeklong celebration featured plays by seven African American companies from different parts of the country, each with roots in the civil rights movement, as well as a performance of Roadside's *South of the Mountain,* in which a white Appalachian family struggles to adapt to a coal-mining economy that extracts a heavy toll on the people and the land while making millionaires out of stockholders in faraway cities.

Junebug and Roadside both worked with the artist-led management and booking agency Holden & Arts Associates, so we sometimes found ourselves on national tours together. On these occasions, the ensembles often traded and improvised stories and songs during workshops and informal performances. The public seemed to like it, so in 1988 Junebug and Roadside decided to write and tour a full joint production: a musical play about the relationship between Black and white poor and working-class people in the South, from the slave trade and the first landing of Scots-Irish indentured servants until the end of the Vietnam War. Our intent was to make it possible for Black and white audiences to see new possibilities for solidarity coming out of the histories and traditions they already knew. In co-creating this play, we came up with a conceptual image that would define all of Roadside's subsequent intercultural partnerships: a bridge, whose span (the new intercultural performance) could be only as strong as the posts on either end were deep (grounded in the cultural history and aesthetic traditions of the respective collaborators' communities).

The Junebug-Roadside play creation started with artists from the two ensembles coming together in New Orleans and Whitesburg to sit in circles and tell each other personal stories about their experience with race, place, and class. Although we had been friends for more than a decade, these circles let us hear one another and ourselves in new ways. From the themes and stories that arose in these circles, we started to create *Junebug/*

Kim Neal Mays and John O'Neal perform Junebug/Jack, *Whitesburg, Kentucky.*
Photo by Jeff Whetstone.

Jack, a dramatic narrative with original music. As was both ensembles' custom, we tested and revised the play with our home audiences before setting about our stock-in-trade: touring. We suggested that potential hosts for our new play ask themselves whether their community was ready to delve into its own history of race and class relationships. If they said they were ready, or just wanted to take a chance, we would take the play there.

Roadside had always taken pains to build touring audiences that reflected communities in their full diversity. Now, touring with Junebug, the specific challenge was how to get large numbers of Black and white working-class and poor people to attend. In the main, such folks didn't hang out together, much less go to see professional theater. After unsuccessfully trying all the tools in our promotional kits, including getting the word out to places like barbershops and bars, we hit on a new idea: Every community wishing to present *Junebug/Jack* would have to agree to form an ecumenical community chorus. This chorus would include singers from the Black and white churches, and perhaps from the local women's chorus or the high school glee club. It was the community sponsor's job to talk singers into joining up, which itself often took some bridge-building work. Each newly minted chorus received the music several months before we arrived, and a few days before the opening performance we staged the singers into the show. They didn't sign up to discuss race and class—they signed up to sing, and this professional play looked like a good opportunity to shine. Yet while rehearsing the music, they naturally hit on a sound they had never heard before: Voices from across the community joined to sing beautiful songs drawn from southern Black and white traditions, about a four-hundred-year-old struggle that had often pitted them against each other. The excitement of rehearsals quickly spread through singers' families and schools and congregations, and on opening night a full cross section of the community was present.

In the days following performances of *Junebug/Jack*, audience members were invited to mimic the process we had used to create the play: to sit together in circles and share personal stories about race and class in their lives and their community. Having experienced the frankness of the performance together, in which no individual or group was made into a villain or victim or savior, they felt a newfound freedom to tell one another stories that were complex, challenging, and emotional, and rarely told in "mixed" company. One night in eastern Mississippi, a white woman in the circle told of a Black woman who took care of her when she was a small child: "I loved my nanny, and I was heartbroken when

Roadside Theater, Junebug Productions, and a community chorus perform Junebug/Jack, *1997. Photo courtesy Roadside Theater.*

she suddenly stopped coming to my house." Crying, she continued: "Throughout my childhood, I feared that I had done something wrong and she had abandoned me." As we continued around the circle, a Black man told a story about his mother: "My mother spent six days and six nights every week taking care of a white child so we could have a roof over our heads and food on the table." By the end of the evening, they discovered they were talking about the same person, that his mother was her nanny. He said, "For so many years I hated this child I had never met, because she took my mother away from me. Now I see that this situation harmed her, too." Another participant that night likened this moment to a painting in which light from heaven flooded the circle.

Witnessing the impact of the play and the depth of community involvement that was possible, Roadside, Junebug, and Holden & Arts Associates began developing a multiyear community residency program specifically around matters of race and class. As with Roadside's previous community cultural development residencies, we did not solicit communities, but waited for them to invite us in. We agreed on three guiding principles: (1) active participation, with no bystanders, including the residency's private and public funders; (2) partnerships and collaborations with an inclusive range of community organizations, and with no in-crowds or out-groups; and (3) diverse local leadership, with no hierarchy based on race, gender, or class. Our goal was to leave behind a broad and organized base of citizens who would carry on the work we'd started together, long after we left.

A residency typically began with performances of *Junebug/Jack*. Then in workshops with community members, we explained and illustrated the play-creation process, including the central role of stories. We knew that stories possessed immense power, which could be used for good or ill: The stories we can tell, imagine, and understand are what define our sense of who we are, what has happened in the past, and what is possible in the future. To harness the democratic power of stories, and stop them from being used to dominate and exploit, we developed a formal protocol for what we called "story circles." Participants sat in a circle, in a quiet place with no distractions. Each person told a personal story based on a mutually agreed-upon theme, one by one, while everyone else listened. A facilitator emphasized that the group would be telling stories—with characters, a setting, conflict, and a beginning and end—not making speeches, presenting arguments, or offering commentary. No one could join a story circle late, and everyone agreed to participate. Each person was asked to tell a story of approximately the same length—the length having been calculated by the amount of time available divided by the number of participants, with time set aside at the end for reflection.

The experience began when the facilitator reiterated the prompt, the group shared a moment of silence, and someone spoke up to tell the first story. Next came the person to the previous teller's right, who could either tell a story or pass; for people who passed, their turn would come around again. Even if someone told a controversial story, there was no cross talk in response; participants would have the chance to respond in the form of their own stories when it was their turn. Naturally, when the circle's agreed-upon theme was announced, many participants would immediately begin thinking about what story they were going to tell. Facilitators encouraged people *not* to share that one, and instead to wait and

Story circle at the annual meeting of the Performing Our Future coalition, including Roadside ensemble members and community leaders and organizers from Baltimore, Maryland; Uniontown, Alabama; Milwaukee and Sauk County, Wisconsin; and Letcher County, Kentucky. Arch Social Club, Baltimore, Maryland, 2020. Photo by Adam Carr.

listen until it was their turn, then offer a personal story that responded to, elaborated upon, or contradicted the other stories they had heard so far. After each participant had told a story, the group thought together about what had just happened. Which stories were similar? Which were strikingly different? What had everyone learned? Had a new, collective "story in the middle of the circle" begun to take shape? What theme or topic would the group like to pursue in its next circle?

By learning how to convene, facilitate, and participate in story circles, residents began to appreciate one another and discover the richness and complexity of their own community's life. The stories (and occasionally songs) that emerged from the circles, which were recorded when there was unanimous consent, became the basic ingredients for celebratory community events, often potluck suppers, at which participants shared the stories and songs they had now begun to craft. Nascent and experienced community playwrights, producers, directors, actors, and designers used this expanding body of local expression to develop performances connected to issues involving race and class. The Roadside-Junebug-Holden team continued to learn when to lead and when to follow, taking care to step in only to teach a skill or fill a gap of inexperience.

These residencies were our deepest and fullest work yet, in long-term collaboration with communities to address their toughest problems. And it was here that the work came up against obstacles we could not always surmount. Two years into a project in a small city in eastern North Carolina, the city's Black and white communities had just presented their first play, and the residency already had another year of funding committed from the state arts council. The next step was to work with project leaders to create the organizational infrastructure to sustain the work. But the majority of the community's white leaders balked at creating a formal structure where they would share decision making with their Black collaborators. Other project partners were unable to change the white leaders' minds, leaving Junebug and Roadside with no choice but to withdraw from the project and send back the remaining state arts money. As in all of our projects, we worked with residents to document their successes and analyze the barriers they encountered, in the hope that future local leaders might pick up where we'd left off.

In the Dayton Stories residency in Ohio, more than one hundred race and class story circles were conducted over the course of a year, with many of the recordings archived by Dayton's Montgomery County Historical Society. This material became the basis for two popular main-stage plays and a contemporary dance performance. One of these plays, developed by the city's largest professional theater, was selected by regional critics as the year's best drama. Afterward, when we asked the theater's leaders about their plans for next season's local play, they laughed and said there was no plan—the process had taken up too much staff time and too much money! Sure enough, the following year's season was picked from the national pool of already successfully produced plays. As public funding continued to decline, we would again and again see democratic participation and creativity derailed not only by explicit racism but also by the subtler barriers of bureaucratic efficiency.

● ● ●

As we became more and more aware of the threats circling around our work, the Roadside-Junebug-Holden team kept an eye out for opportunities to build an even broader network of allies. The cofounding of Alternate ROOTS in 1976 had been an ambitious start, but at the big biennial festival six years later, we looked out at the audience and realized it was artists performing for other artists: the whole community was no longer present.

Later that year, at the 1982 People's Theater Festival in San Francisco, Roadside and Junebug cofounded a new coalition: the multicultural American Festival Project, which in the following years grew to include A Traveling Jewish Theatre from San Francisco; Pregones Theater from the South Bronx; Urban Bush Women, based in New York City; Idiwanan An Chawe from Zuni Pueblo, New Mexico; Carpetbag Theatre from Knoxville, Tennessee; El Teatro de la Esperanza from Oakland; Liz Lerman Dance Exchange, based in Washington, D.C.; Robbie McCauley & Company from Boston; Francisco González y su Conjunto from Southern California; and Jessica Hagedorn and Company, based in New York City. Each of these ensembles created performances rooted in the cultural life of its community, including its issues of race and class; each had a national reputation for artistic excellence; and each was committed to supporting a broad-based people's movement toward democracy.

In its twenty-five years of existence, the American Festival Project produced twenty-one festivals across the country, working at a scale that's difficult for many of us to imagine today. Festivals typically occurred over a two- to five-year period, coproduced by Holden & Arts Associates and one or more local organizations. Two festivals, the 1991–1992 Mississippi festival and the 1992–1995 Montana festival, took place across an entire state; others took place across cities, towns, and rural areas. Festivals included coalition ensembles presenting their new theater, dance, and musical work, both individually and in various combinations, as well as new performances created in collaboration with artists and justice-oriented organizations in the host communities.

A milestone of the four-year Ithaca/Cornell American Festival was a ten-day celebration in 1989 to open the university's new Schwartz Center for the Performing Arts: Ten American Festival dance, music, and

Roadside Theater and Urban Bush Women perform at the Open Windows Festival, part of the American Festival Project, Whitesburg, Kentucky, 1988. Photo by Jeff Whetstone.

theater ensembles performed in the center's four new theaters and took part in a meeting with thirty scholars of various races and ethnicities on the role of the humanities in a multicultural nation. During their stay, American Festival artists conducted more than seventy workshops and performances in the county's community centers, churches, and schools. And on their travels back home, many of these artists stopped off to visit communities that held a special meaning for them: Francisco González y su Conjunto visited the camps of migrant laborers picking the fall apples, and Roadside spent several days exchanging stories, playing music, and dancing with the Akwesasne Mohawk community.

Three years later, in 1992, the three-day conference Grassroots Theater in Historical and Contemporary Perspective brought one hundred community artists and scholars from across the country to Cornell and resulted in the publication of *From the Ground Up,* now used as a textbook to teach the history of people's theater in the United States. Robert Gard, born in 1910, came back to his alma mater to give his last public address to the field of grassroots theater. (When Roadside contacted Gard with the invitation, he replied, "I've been waiting for someone to come, and wondering if they would.") Gard was one of five keynote speakers, along with Peter Jemison, Seneca artist and educator; William Branch, African American playwright and scholar; Nicolás Kanellos, scholar of Hispanic theater; and Lorraine Brown, white historian of the Federal Theatre Project. Presented in historical sequence, from before the arrival of Europeans to the closing of the Federal Theatre Project, these five keynote speakers bore witness to the enduring democratic impulse in the performing arts, and the desire of grassroots artists to work across barriers of race and class. They also offered a grim reminder of how those in power had ensured such a united cultural front did not form.

That same year, the 1992 Dartmouth American Festival offered Roadside new insight into our role as a white organization within a multicultural coalition. At the festival's opening reception, visiting artists, student leaders, sponsoring faculty, and guests grabbed food and drinks and coalesced into animated groups. Before long, Native American students proudly led the Festival's Oklahoma Indian Theater and Dance Company to a more intimate gathering at their Native American House. Soon after, Junebug artists left for a dinner in their honor hosted by Dartmouth's Black Caucus, and El Teatro de la Esperanza departed with members of MEChA and La Alianza Latina. When Hillel gathered up A Traveling Jewish Theatre, Roadside experienced that sinking feeling familiar to every child—and to all the festival's other artists at so many moments in their lives—of not having been picked. Practically alone now at the once buzzing party, we said good night to the few lingering faculty members, shuffled back to the Hanover Inn, and called a company meeting. The meeting had one agenda item: Who on this campus is like us?

The next morning, we found the answer hiding in plain sight: the crews clearing snow, doing maintenance work, cooking in the cafeteria kitchen, and staffing the lower tiers of the administrative offices. (Just like back home in the mountains, the working class in rural New Hampshire was overwhelmingly white.) The workers at the Hopkins Center for the Arts told us that although they helped produce scores of performance events each year, they rarely attended any of them. With a nudge from our

Dartmouth sponsors, campus service workers were given the option of "work release" to participate in festival events as members of Roadside's official host committee. It was an eyepopper for students and faculty when we arrived with our posse for the interdepartmental seminar Cultural Appropriation and First Voice. Roadside and the service staff held daily storytelling sessions, and students slowly started joining us, each surprised not to be the only poor student there. Everyone knew Dartmouth had one of the wealthiest student bodies in the United States, and we laughed and cried together at the students' stories of leading double lives, detailing their ever-more-elaborate stratagems to explain to their classmates why they couldn't go on the ski trip this coming weekend or down to the party in Boston the week after.

Roadside continued working with institutions of higher education in the following decades. Our goal, as ever, was to broaden our base. Among the thousands of students preparing for careers in the performing arts, we reasoned, some of them must be ready to escape the straitjacket of mass-consumer performance, if we could show them it was possible. Roadside's 2001–2002 course Grassroots Theater in Theory & Practice at NYU's Tisch School of the Arts ended up providing thirty such students with a pointed lesson in a basic principle of our work: the importance of understanding ourselves and our institutions as part of the surrounding community and recognizing the role we play in the community's problems. After initial training in story circles and oral history collection, the students went forth to learn about their community's worries and hopes. The idea was that students would work with the people they interviewed to devise new plays based on the stories they collected and then perform them with community members in neighborhood venues.

But as it turned out, the neighborhood's chief concern was NYU itself, specifically the gentrification being propelled by the university's rapid expansion. This gentrification, the students soon realized, was being underwritten by their tuition checks, which would, in turn, keep many of them in debt for years or even decades to come. These realizations caused an abrupt change of course. The students began digging into NYU's less than transparent financial history, aided by several allies on the NYU faculty. With their research and stories in hand, students created lively and often humorous performances that would pop up wherever their Tisch classmates gathered to relax, with nonuniversity neighbors present as witnesses.

When we left campus at the end of these kinds of projects, our sadness wasn't just about parting ways with our newfound friends. No matter how close our collaborators had grown, and how beautiful and important the theater they had made during our time together, we knew from experience that these bonds and this work were unlikely to be sustained. The institutions we left behind would not invest the necessary resources to keep the work going, and in the end the status quo returned. Not for the first time or the last, we observed that the field of democratic arts was littered with the corpses of its successes.

● ● ●

Since the 1970s, Roadside had kept a close eye on research coming out of the Highlander Center, detailing how our central Appalachian home had been thrust into the throes of globalization before most people knew the word. We had essentially become a mineral colony of multinational energy corporations, a fate we shared with communities around the world.

In 1987, Roadside joined with the Caribbean Cultural Center Africa Diaspora Institute in New York City to study these dynamics and connections, and in 1993 we collaborated to organize the Global Network for Cultural Equity. The network's inaugural publication, *Voices from the Battlefront: Achieving Cultural Equity,* featured sixteen essays drawn from a series of three international conferences collectively entitled Cultural Diversity Based on Cultural Grounding. Participants in these conferences recognized culture's critical role in global development: Exploitative development depends on a culture of top-down administration and control, and equitable development depends on a culture of bottom-up collective power. For this reason, they argued, the struggle for cultural equity would define the twenty-first century, much as the struggle against racism had helped define the twentieth century. Roadside participated in these conferences alongside colleagues from around the world, sharing our coal mining region's experience with race, class, land, and the exploitative dynamics of the global energy economy, and committing to the shared work of creating a level playing field on which all the world's cultures had equal opportunity to develop.

Roadside also built international alliances through touring, starting with a 1985 engagement with Junebug and A Traveling Jewish Theatre at the Other America Festival in Sweden and Denmark. We struggled to connect with audiences in London, where Margaret Thatcher's funding cuts had closed most of the working-class theaters and left audiences with a superficial and stereotypical view of our culture, much like audiences in the States whose perspective had been shaped by TV shows like *Dallas* and movies like *Deliverance*. But when we left London and went to Wales, it was like coming home. Thatcher's privatization policies had left Welsh mining communities in poverty, in a way that felt strikingly familiar. Hearing hundreds of Welsh voices rising together to sing Florence Reece's "Which Side Are You On?" was unforgettable. (Our tour, sponsored by the British Labour Party in collaboration with the United Mine Workers of America, included performances with the Cardiff-based Red Choir—red being the color of Welsh independence. Not surprisingly, we were under surveillance the entire time.)

We found similar resonance during a four-year exchange with Czech theater artists who had been part of the resistance to communism. Our exchange began shortly after the 1989 Velvet Revolution and included a conversation with playwright turned president Václav Havel. Our Czech collaborators taught us a lot about making art under Communist rule (the Party censor's doorless office was always on the left as you entered a theater). And when we performed with the folk ensemble Hradistan, it was their first public appearance since being forced underground by the Party's ban on all forms of folk expression.

Roadside has also worked for decades with sovereign nations that share our geography. Our collaboration with traditional singers and dancers in Zuni Pueblo began in 1985 and eventually sparked the creation of the first Zuni-language theater company, Idiwanan An Chawe ("Children of the Middle Place"). One of the company's founders was on the team that created a written alphabet to help preserve and perpetuate the Zuni language, Shiwi'ma Bena:we. And the play Roadside and

Elgin Hechilay, Charlene Hechilay, Tommy Bledsoe, Arden Kucate, Kim Neal Mays, and Ron Short perform Corn Mountain/Pine Mountain: Following the Seasons, *Whitesburg, Kentucky, 1998. Photo by Tim Cox.*

Idiwanan An Chawe created together, *Corn Mountain/Pine Mountain: Following the Seasons // Dowa Yalanne/Ashek'ya Yalanne: Debikwayinan Idulohha,* has become the standard text for teaching written Zuni.

The subject of the play was our shared concern about the destruction of our communities' natural environments. The federal government had dammed the Zuni River upstream, crippling the region's farming economy, and now there was a proposal by a private corporation to strip-mine for coal near the sacred Zuni Salt Lake. This was a tale all too familiar to us, living in a place where generations of farmers had been displaced by corporate coal-mining operations, and where strip mining had ravaged the landscape and poisoned the water since the 1950s. The play's cast of six storytellers and up to sixteen traditional Zuni dancers and singers told of the destruction of Mother Earth in both our homes through traditional Zuni and Appalachian songs and stories. *Corn Mountain/Pine Mountain* premiered in Zuni Pueblo and Roadside's home theater in Kentucky in 1996, toured the Southwest, and was featured at the national

Environmental Justice Festival in New Orleans in 1998—seven years before Hurricane Katrina.

The 2002 book *Journeys Home: Revealing a Zuni-Appalachia Collaboration* tells the story of the sixteen-year exchange that led to the play's creation and offers introductions to the history of Zuni Pueblo and central Appalachia and essays about the Zuni language and the Appalachian dialect. It also includes the full side-by-side text of *Corn Mountain/Pine Mountain* in English and Shiwi'ma Bena:we:

The corn grows green	Shetda: ashenan ilenak'ya
And the corn grows tall.	La:ł shetda: a:dasha'a.
The sun shines down	Yadokkya an dek'yałnan baniyu
And the warm rains fall.	Da: łidokkya a:yusu a:baniyu.
New life springs from the old,	Kwa'hoł a:łashshina'kow'annan chim'on a:wiyo'a,
It's something to believe in.	Hish lukkya' iłdemanakya.
And this old world keeps spinning round,	La:ł luk ulohnan łashhina idullapcho,
Sometimes up, sometimes down,	Ishoł kyamana, ishoł manikkyana,
Summer, winter, spring, and fall,	Olo'ik'ya, dehts'ina, delakwayyi, dap miyashe:nak'ya
Following the seasons.	Debikwaynan an haydoshna: wotdaban dina:ne.

More recently, stimulated by our collaboration with Zuni artists, Roadside began working with Native neighbors close to home in Cherokee, North Carolina. Together with southwest Virginia's Natural Tunnel State Park and Daniel Boone Wilderness Trail Association, we drew on local traditions of historical reenactment to create the annual outdoor drama *Stronger Than Blood,* in which a white, African American, and Cherokee cast offers local audiences a more complex than expected journey into local history, told in two languages.

• • •

Yet even as Roadside's international and intercultural ties grew stronger, so did the common threats we were facing. By the 1990s, the regime of privatization promoted by Thatcher and Reagan was spreading nearly unchecked across the globe. In 1995, the National Endowment for the Arts stopped offering grants to individual artists. In 1996, Fox News went live. In 1997, the NEA closed its entire presenting and touring program, as well as its multicultural Expansion Arts Program, a legacy of the Federal Theatre Project and a direct consequence of the civil rights movement. The persistent attacks on the NEA meant the end of local arts councils and the weakening of state and regional arts agencies. Private foundations again followed suit and cut back their support for touring artists and grassroots multicultural organizations, in favor of the large urban institutions preferred by their wealthy trustees and executives. For those of us outside the rising gates of the shrinking nonprofit arts field, imposed scarcity was becoming the order of the day.

By 1999, Roadside's national touring program was effectively bankrupt. The national American Festival coalition managed to hang on a little longer, but it dissolved during the 2008 Great Recession. The Global Network for Cultural Equity could no longer raise the money to bring international grassroots intellectuals and organizations together to study the cultural and economic forces damaging all of our communities. Our shared critical discourse broke down. Many of our colleagues retreated to safer and better-paying jobs away from the front lines, often in higher education. For those who remained, life could be miserable, as onetime allies took their eyes off the prize and fell prey to opportunists who pitted communities and their organizations against each other in a contest to determine who was most deserving of what little was left. (In such circumstances, our friends at Junebug told us, the SNCC saying was, "When people don't have anything to do, they do each other.") For young people entering the work in the new millennium, this was the only reality they knew.

As Roadside faced this newly hostile landscape, we decided to dedicate our remaining resources to continuing our intercultural play creation and residencies, and to projects that addressed the growing emergencies in our communities. Through this work, we hoped to begin rebuilding some of the solidarity, creativity, and critical analysis that had been lost as the public sphere continued to shrink.

The East Bay Center for the Performing Arts in Richmond, California, contacted us in the late 1990s, hoping to use our storytelling-based playmaking process to bring together divided cultural groups in the area known as the Iron Triangle. Roadside and East Bay partners conducted story circles with the area's residents, including the Mexicans who had first settled the land, the African American and white residents (including some from Appalachia) who had come to Richmond to work in the shipyards during World War II, and the Laotian Iu Mien refugees from the Vietnam War. (One of Roadside's ensemble members who had fought in Vietnam found particular alliance and communion with the Iu Mien, the project's other mountain people. They had similar stories of farming, freedom, and strong family ties, before industrialization and war upended their world.) Months of story circles, intercultural dialogues, shared meals, and late-night libations featuring Mien and Kentucky moonshine culminated in round-robin performances and traditional meals in a Mien cultural center, a Hispanic cultural center, and an African American Baptist church. These events took on the working title *Stranger at the Table,* reflecting the group's shared conviction: "Never start a political dialogue on an empty stomach!" And in the East Bay Cultural Center, Roadside found a partner that would continue and build upon our work in the years that followed.

Meanwhile on the East Coast, Roadside had long observed southern Appalachia playing tag with the South Bronx at the bottom of the federal government's annual poverty reports, and we reasoned that Bronx theater artists might be our long-lost thespian cousins. We got the chance to find out in 1994, when the South Bronx–based Puerto Rican theater Pregones invited us to perform in their venue, a converted mattress factory. (Pregones cleverly advertised our visit as *The Mountains Come to the Bronx!* without mentioning that the coming mountains were not, in fact, Puerto Rican.) Our early joint performances typically started with Roadside telling a traditional tale like "Jack and the Giant Killer," followed by Pregones telling one of their own from the same genre, like "Juan Bobo Refuses to Marry the Princess." Then the ensembles' musicians would kick in with cuatro, banjo, and fiddle, and audiences in Kentucky and the Bronx alike would be on their feet, dancing. Before long Junebug wanted in on the action, so we expanded our circuit to include New Orleans.

The excitement generated by these gatherings propelled the three companies to create a new musical play, *Promise of a Love Song*. It premiered in 1999, two years after the NEA cutbacks; to scrape together the resources for the project, Holden & Arts Associates recruited co-commissioners and presenting partners in nine states. But even with all this support, and a play that proved popular with audiences, we were only able to mount a modest tour. National touring, the mainstay of Roadside's economy since 1978, was over.

While *Promise of a Love Song* depicted the common quest for love from the perspective of three distinct and often conflicting cultures, Roadside and Pregones's next joint project—*Betsy!*—embodied these conflicts within a single character: a proud young Puerto Rican jazz singer who discovers, much to her dismay, that she is also descended from Scots-Irish indentured servants in Appalachia. (The play's relevance was underlined by a mobile unit parked a few blocks from our rehearsal space in the Bronx that advertised *DNA TESTING—Who's Your Daddy?*) Just months after *Betsy!* closed Off-Broadway, the megahit *Hamilton* opened a few blocks away. The contrast between the two musicals could not have been clearer; both were stories of Caribbean immigrants making their way in the United States, but where one celebrates its protagonist's "rise up" into the nation's financial and political elite, the other delves deep into the complex multiracial underclass that Hamilton and his followers helped create.

Touring *Betsy!* was never even discussed as a possibility, though we did bring a scaled-down version to Appalachia in 2017. But by that point, we had lost a lot of our local audience, too. The bottom had dropped out of the economy as machines replaced miners, natural gas replaced coal, and younger generations fled the area in search of work. Those who remained were often disabled from mining-related injuries and illnesses like black lung. A generation had fallen prey to opioids, dumped on the region by the pharmaceutical industry. The congressional district that includes Roadside's home base of Letcher County, Kentucky, was declared one of the worst places in the United States to live, based on levels of poverty, disease, suicide, drug addiction, and mortality rates. It was in this context that two maximum-security prisons were built on nearby abandoned strip-mining sites and sold to the public as engines of economic growth. Most of the prisoners at Wallens Ridge and Red Onion were Black, imported from distant cities, and typically kept in lockdown twenty-three hours a day. It was not unusual for them to go years without a visit from a loved one.

These prisoners and guards and their families were new neighbors, and Roadside set about collecting their stories. We learned that "shooting a kite" was prison slang for sending a message, so the play we made from these stories took on the name *Thousand Kites*. The play has three acts, without an intermission. Act 1 is a performance or reading of the forty-five-minute-long script, with its nine characters typically played by former prisoners, former corrections officers, and their respective family members. When productions started happening elsewhere, cast members were encouraged to swap out parts of the script for their own stories and spoken word compositions, working with a Roadside director to keep the play's general flow and structure intact. Act 2 turned to the audience: With smaller audiences, each cast member facilitated a story circle; with larger crowds, performers asked for testimonies from audience members. In Act 3, the audience was asked to imagine actions that could do something about the realities they had just witnessed. Like other Roadside plays tackling a particular community issue, *Thousand Kites* was made available royalty-free on the internet, along with instructions about how to produce it. In the following years, we heard from scores of organizations across the country that were using the play in their prison-reform campaigns. Eventually, the play became part of a national multimedia organizing campaign for prison reform called Nation Inside, coordinated by a former Roadside ensemble member.

· · ·

Organizing, the process of ordinary people and community organizations building the shared power to act together across differences, became an ever-more-central aspect of Roadside's work as the situation around us grew more dire. Our decades working with Junebug brought us into close contact with civil rights veterans, and a 1999–2002 project in California gave us the chance to collaborate with affiliates of the Industrial Areas Foundation, the organizing network founded by Saul Alinsky. Our work back home also put us in touch with generations of coal miners and their families who had organized with the United Mine Workers of America, one of the first successful multiracial unions, which became the backbone of the 1930s labor movement.

But as imposed scarcity took its toll on our communities, local traditions of solidarity were being eroded. Back in 1931, Florence Reece sang "Which Side Are You On?" to implore listeners to support their loved ones working in the mines against the bosses who were exploiting them. But eighty years later, when a powerful Kentucky senator and his allies asked the same question, the sides had shifted: Now you could either be "pro-coal," which meant pro-corporation, pro-exploitation, and pro-pollution; or "anti-coal," which meant against everyone's loved ones who had given their lives in the mines to keep their families from going hungry. Heads the bosses win; tails the workers lose.

Could a play do something to address this kind of situation, where economic despair was being weaponized to break the ability of communities to organize themselves? To answer this question, Roadside began a new community cultural development residency in our home county, which would deepen our understanding of the connections between grassroots theater, organizing, and economic development. Together with a team of organizers and development economists, we came up with a hypothesis: Through creating a play together about their economic future, a community's residents could resist the divide-and-conquer strategy of their exploiters, tell new stories that "unbound their imaginations," and discover new sources of economic value (or "latent assets") in their communities, which they could turn into community-owned wealth. Part of our work was learning the vocabulary of organizing and development economics, integrating it with the jargon of our own field, and building a lexicon for what we started calling "community cultural and economic development."

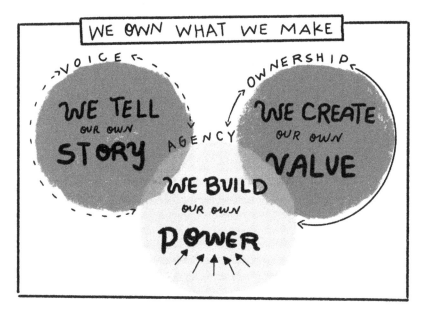

WE OWN WHAT WE MAKE

VOICE

OWNERSHIP

WE TELL
OUR OWN
STORY

AGENCY

WE CREATE
OUR OWN
VALUE

WE BUILD
OUR OWN
POWER

Diagram showing Roadside Theater's approach to "community cultural and economic development"—a synergistic practice of grassroots cultural work, broad-based community organizing, and community wealth creation. Artwork by Kate Fowler.

For the first time, a Roadside community cultural development project was led not by a theater producer but by an organizer with a background in theater. In some ways it was a standard Roadside residency: A playwright and a team of local youth set out across the county, conducting interviews and leading story circles, which became the basis of a new play called *The Future of Letcher County*. But this time, alongside the playmaking process ran an organizing process: mapping out the community's power structures, identifying and building relationships with grassroots leaders, discovering mutual self-interest and building a shared agenda, and ultimately creating a coalition that became known as the Letcher County Culture Hub, made up of the county's community centers, volunteer fire departments, artist/artisan associations, small businesses, and other locally led groups.

These kinds of organizations, where ordinary people are in charge and everyone is welcome to participate, are what Roadside calls "community centers of power." (The term is derived from civil rights strategist

Bayard Rustin, who in his 1965 essay "From Protest to Politics" called for "the building of community institutions or power bases.") Community centers of power, by their nature, are both solidly rooted in their own communities and always looking outward for allies and collaborators. In the case of the Culture Hub, leaders from eighteen local organizations ended up meeting frequently to share stories and work together on projects that would benefit their own residents and build a grassroots base. These projects included reviving the state's oldest square dance, founding a brick-oven bakery run by former drug dealers and employing local residents coming back from prison, and building the area's largest non-industrial solar energy project. They also became the cast of *The Future of Letcher County,* in performances at home and away.

Roadside's last live engagement before the coronavirus pandemic was a performance of *The Future of Letcher County* at the Arch Social Club, the oldest African American social organization in West Baltimore. The Arch and the Culture Hub represented communities on opposite ends of the nation's racial, political, and rural-urban divides, yet they quickly saw themselves in each other. Early on in the performance, a Trump-loving Letcher County volunteer fire chief, who played the equally conservative character Harlan, went off script and talked about the Narcan kit by the front door of the Arch; hardly a weekend went by back home when he and his fellow firefighters didn't use this same emergency medicine to save the lives of neighbors who had overdosed on opioids. An audience member responded, "I didn't realize white people had those problems, too."

The leaders of the Arch and the Culture Hub realized they were both looking to build community networks where ordinary people could tell their own stories, build their own power, and create their own value. The ultimate goal was a future where the community could say "We own what we make." This phrase started out as the Culture Hub's tagline, and it was soon also adopted by the Arch, by a multicultural group of "cultural and agricultural producers" in Wisconsin called Rural Urban Flow, and by a civil rights organization in rural Alabama called Black Belt Citizens Fighting for Health and Justice. These four unlikely collaborators met together for the first time in 2018 in Uniontown, Alabama, where they quickly saw how similar and interconnected their stories were. Black Belt

Denise Griffin Johnson, director of the Arch Social Community Network in West Baltimore, jokes with Bill Meade, chief of the Kings Creek Volunteer Fire Department in Letcher County, Kentucky, during a break at the annual meeting of the Performing Our Future coalition, Arch Social Club, Baltimore, Maryland, 2020. Photo by Ben Fink.

Citizens took everyone to see the seven-story mountain of coal ash that had been dumped in residents' backyards, which was now poisoning the local water supply—and which had its origins in the Scotia Mine, site of the deadliest coal mine explosion in the history of Letcher County.

The message was clear: Our exploiters are organized and united, and we must be, too. This was the same message that had been passed down from the Farmers Alliance and the People's Party of the 1880s–1890s (the original Populists) to the labor movement of the 1930s, then to the civil rights movement of the 1960s, and now to us. Roadside had always located ourselves in the populist tradition, but this new project added new dimensions to that commitment. The coalition that began at that meeting in Alabama, which took the name Performing Our Future, resembled Roadside's past multicultural and intercultural initiatives in that the work was grounded in its community stories and traditions; its work began by people in each place spending time in one another's communities, sharing stories and performances, and discovering opportunities to make meaningful and beautiful things together. But in other ways this grouping was something new: It was a coalition not of performance ensembles, but of community centers of power, led by grassroots leaders and organizers who worked closely with artists and understood that political change lies downstream of cultural change.

As individual delegations and as a coalition, Performing Our Future worked at the places where communities butted up against the organized interests that kept them down, working explicitly to build the cultural, political, and economic power necessary to make structural change. Powerful stories told by ordinary people fueled not only community plays and performances but also environmental studies, voter registration and education campaigns, cross-partisan dialogues, rural-urban bus tours, agricultural and food exchanges, and partnerships to start cooperative businesses. Roadside continues to hope that such a coalition may be able to confront the anti-democratic policies and attitudes that had been building for decades, and which had blocked our past projects from achieving their ultimate goal: a nationwide network of grassroots communities with the power and vision to realize the unfulfilled ideal of art in a democracy.

●　●　●

As Roadside looks back at forty-five years on the road, and forward into the third decade of a new millennium, three big questions remain on our minds. Can the people's work be supported by the people's money? Can communities struggling against exploitation build cultural, political, and economic power together? And finally: Will we maintain the patience, discipline, and energy to support one another and be ready when the next movement comes?

Can the people's work be supported by the people's money? It is difficult to imagine art in a democracy without significant public support. Roadside's early years were made possible not only by the National Endowment for the Arts but also by the federal Comprehensive Employment and Training Act (CETA), which paid many ensemble members' salaries. Inspired by the 1930s WPA and passed during the Nixon administration,

CETA offered publicly funded jobs that served the community. Several years later, Jimmy Carter's Department of Housing and Urban Development (HUD) appointed community organizer Monsignor Geno Baroni to launch the Neighborhood Self-Help Program. Understanding that ordinary residents were best equipped to take the lead in addressing their own challenges and opportunities, this program offered flexible, open-ended assistance to community centers of power. Reagan quickly shut down both programs. But they show what's possible when government makes a large-scale investment of people's tax dollars directly into the places where people live and work together. There is no reason this cannot happen again.

Can communities struggling against exploitation build cultural, political, and economic power together? Today, forces from across the political spectrum call on us to make a fetish of our differences: racist pseudo-populism on the Right, ideological cliquishness on the Left, and generic identity politics in the center. The orchestrated demise of so many of our communities' centers of power has made these divisive calls ever harder to resist. Yet here, as always, we can learn from those who came before us. Junebug's John O'Neal often said he wished he had a hundred dollars for each time a well-intentioned white liberal confidently sidled up to him and opined that if we could only get rid of the rednecks, we could move ahead as a country. They were dumbfounded when he replied, "Those white rednecks you speak of are some of my closest allies."

Will we maintain the patience, discipline, and energy to support one another and be ready when the next movement comes? Movements are the times we all wait for. When the dam bursts, all manner of unexpected allies jump on board, and big changes seem suddenly within reach. Our current social media-saturated moment is full of prematurely declared "movements," which turn out to be factional protest groups without enough public support to make lasting change. Genuine movements, as the late Myles Horton of the Highlander Center often observed, are few and far between. We spend most of our lives in what he called "organizational periods": the challenging in-between times, when smaller numbers of allies develop leaders, build power, win victories as we can, and maintain the organizations and relationships that will form the backbone of future movements. Being ready when the next movement comes means creating the conditions for a critical mass of people and communities to see themselves in a common struggle for freedom and dignity. And this, ultimately, has always been Roadside Theater's intention: to affirm the value of each person's unique story and every community's distinctive material, intellectual, spiritual, and emotional life; and to reveal the incomparable beauty and power of coming together in communion with neighbors near and far.

A Note About Language and Dialect

PHAEDRUS: You mean the living word of knowledge which has a soul, and of which the written word is properly no more than an image?

SOCRATES: Yes, of course that is what I mean.

Whether at home in the mountains or on national tour, the Roadside ensemble has always appreciated the detailed attention our audiences pay to our work. At intermission in 1978 at the Manhattan Theatre Club in New York, two theater mavens were reviewing our play's first act: "Certainly the most authentic of the various Appalachian accents we've heard."

In our story swapping with audiences after shows, the actors sometimes sensed that people were waiting for them to drop their presumably practiced Appalachian accent. On at least one occasion, an audience member came right out with it: "I've always been fascinated by the craft of acting. How long after a performance does it take for you to resume talking like yourself?"

What such audience members missed, or might not have believed, was that all Roadside performers were raised in a small cluster of counties in central Appalachia, and their dialect was natural. If they had to learn anything, it was how to speak so-called standard English!

In his essay "Guilt and the Past Participle: True Confessions from the Appalachian Diaspora," published in the Roadside–Idiwanan An Chawe book *Journeys Home: Revealing a Zuni-Appalachia Collaboration,* Tony Earley begins: "Although my wife, Sarah, and I grew up outside of the same small town in western North Carolina and attended the same public schools, the differences in our backgrounds can make our marriage a surprisingly cross-cultural institution. Simply put, Sarah's grandfather owned a textile mill; mine owned a mule."

Earley goes on to confess: "Although the years I spent in college and graduate school, as well as the upwardly mobile pretentions I acquired along the way, have erased most of the superficial social differences between Sarah and me, the subject of class comes up surprisingly often in our day-to-day lives, most often regarding the manner in which I speak when I'm not paying particular attention to the manner in which I speak. Like a lot of people of rural Appalachian descent, I tend to use the past-tense forms of irregular verbs in places where the past-participle form is called for by the grammar books. For example, I'm more likely to say, 'I could have wrote more,' than 'I could have written more,' which happens to be correct. Class distinction, socio-economic disparity, and the cultural history of the Appalachian region become conversational topics whenever Sarah corrects me. I say, 'I should have threw that away.' Sarah says, 'Thrown.' I say, 'Don't tell me how to talk.' In our household the sentence 'I'm going to lay down and take me a nap' is as likely to lead to an impassioned recitation of how my grandfather had to turn to moonshining to feed his family during the Great Depression as it is to my ever getting to sleep."

The four plays in this second volume of the anthology are intercultural collaborations. Two of the plays are bilingual: *Promise of a Love Song* and *Betsy!* The amount of Spanish spoken onstage depends on who is in the audience: When performing *Promise of a Love Song* or *Betsy!* more Spanish is spoken when the majority of the audience is Spanish-speaking. In volume 2's other two plays, *Junebug/Jack* and *Thousand Kites,* African American Vernacular English is spoken by actors who are themselves part of that culture. To get a true sense of the way all this rich language sounds, you might take a look at some of the Roadside performances preserved on video at roadside.org. But in the printed versions of these four plays, there's likely enough Spanish and varieties of Black and Appalachian English for readers to hear these languages' and dialects' distinct music.

People interested in more language exploration may wish to take a look at two other scripts not included in this volume: (1) *Mil Cometas,* Pregones artistic director Rosalba Rolón's Spanish translation of *Thousand Kites,* available at roadside.org; (2) the complete side-by-side English and Zuni text of the Roadside–Idiwanan An Chawe play *Corn Mountain/ Pine Mountain: Following the Seasons // Dowa Yalanne/Ashek'ya Yalanne: Debikwayinan Idulohha,* available in the book *Journeys Home: Revealing a Zuni-Appalachia Collaboration.* To our surprise, that script, replete with its archetypal Zuni and Appalachian tales, has become the standard text for teaching written Zuni, which existed only in the oral tradition until the mid-1970s, when the Shiwi'ma Bena:we alphabet was created.

John O'Neal, 1940–2019

A. B. Spellman

One bright day in 1980, John O'Neal stepped into my office at the National Endowment for the Arts (NEA) and told me, "A. B., I need a grant to bury the Free Southern Theater." I laughed heartily at this obvious joke. The Free Southern Theater (FST) was foundational in the program that I ran, NEA's Expansion Arts Program; of the arts in Black America; of the culture of the South and of New Orleans, its home. I knew the FST was having money problems, but what organizations in the ExArts world didn't have money problems? Finding ways for them to get out of murderous debt was the central challenge of my job. "Sit down," I said; "we'll find a way to save it."

He sat. "No," he replied, "we won't. The Free Southern Theater has been saved enough times already. I want to close it down, collect all of its documents and place them somewhere appropriate, probably Tulane, hold a conference and festival where we get together as many of the people who comprised the theater and its operations, film performances of its repertoire, talk about our memories of it, record all of that, and then hold a New Orleans funeral for the FST as we parade its corpse through the city and then bury it in the ground."

It turned out to be one of the best grants Expansion Arts ever made. Most small or midsize arts organizations don't prepare for their dissolution. They dissipate in administrative and programmatic excruciation until there is nothing left of them. John wasn't having that. He thought that the Free Southern Theater deserved to die with dignity, and that the coming generations of arts activists should have easy access to its bones.

Expansion Arts

This essay isn't about me, so I will be brief with this section. From the 1970s until the century's end, there existed a loose but recognizable coalition of arts activists and organizations that housed them. These artists and their organizations worked in communities that I once described as culture-rich but institution-poor—that is, communities of color, unassimilated ethnic communities, rural and low-income and disabled communities, etc. Most were fairly young organizations. Many started in or after the 1960s, though some traced their origins as far back as the settlement house movement of the late nineteenth and early twentieth centuries and the Works Progress Administration and other Roosevelt-era initiatives.

It became abundantly clear that these artists and the organizations they led needed to come together. In those days, there were no conferences that intersected the cultural lines, no confabulations where the voices of the cultures could speak across the barricades. Open Dialogue was that assembly. The cultures met; they broke into affinity sessions wherein each group defined their issues and brought them back to the big group. Common issues were the business of the whole, and the whole supported the unique causes of particular groups. Open Dialogue continued for many decades.

The Free Southern Theater was relatively senior among these organizations. It originated in 1963, a few years before the Black Arts Movement, La Raza, the rural arts movement, the Asian American arts movement, and others. Vantile Whitfield, the first director of the Expansion Arts Program, traveled the country and found these organizations, identified their common features, organized categories of funding that accommodated those features, and propagated the program and its principles. I became director of Expansion Arts in 1978 and managed to hold it together until the middle of the Clinton administration, when the evangelical Right proclaimed the NEA heathen and sinful and raised millions of dollars waving around pictures it considered pornographic or satanic.

The Right never was able to eliminate the NEA, but they did achieve annual cuts that reduced the agency to near irrelevance. These cuts led to a reorganization of the agency, including an elimination of discipline or field-defined programs, and the end of Expansion Arts.

But the capital *P* Politics were never the central problem for Expansion Arts. To be sure, we always had to convince each new chairman that her or his life would be much easier without hardball inquiries from the Black and Hispanic congressional caucuses. The leaders of the field were not at all shy about jacking up the new chairmen to make sure ExArts continued and to grow its budget, though I can say honestly that I never asked them to do so, as a matter of principle. And we could always show that we could make grants in congressional districts that the programs with the large institutions never could reach.

No, our major opposition came from the "fine" arts world, which denied that there was art of any merit in Expansion Arts and saw the program's budget as a waste of money. Give the money to us, they whined, and we can serve those "culturally deprived" (a vile term) communities better with our outreach. People who would never go to the South Bronx to see a play by Pregones, or to Lowndes County, Alabama, to see a production of the Free Southern Theater, or to Whitesburg, Kentucky, to see Roadside at work had no compunction about screaming "inferior" at us in all their exalted ignorance.

Neutralizing these voices was, perhaps, the most important work that I did.

John O'Neal

John Milton O'Neal, Jr., was born on September 25, 1940, in Mound City, Illinois, to schoolteacher parents. He attended Southern Illinois University and graduated with a double major in English and philosophy. John's life after graduation was all activism. He took a job with the United Church of Christ's Commission for Racial Justice. From there, he joined the Congress of Racial Equality (CORE), and from CORE moved to the Student Nonviolent Coordinating Committee (SNCC), the most uncompromising of the southern civil rights organizations, where he became a field secretary in Georgia and Mississippi.

COFO, the Council of Federated Organizations, proclaimed a Freedom Summer in Mississippi in 1964. COFO comprised the NAACP, SNCC, and CORE, and most of its staff were SNCC workers, including John. He was based at Tougaloo College, working for SNCC on an adult literacy project that was intended to qualify African Americans to pass the Jim Crow literacy requirements that were then in place in Mississippi.

One fateful evening, John, his SNCC colleague Doris Derby, and his housemate Gilbert Moses were sitting and talking about their frustration with the suppression of cultural expression in Mississippi. They had long advocated a cultural arm for SNCC and thought this would be the time to act. All three were theater people to some degree. John had planned to move to New York and join the Lower Manhattan theater scene before he came south and became a movement worker. Moses was a writer for the Mississippi Free Press and had been trained as an actor at Karamu House in Cleveland, a storied organization that deserves its own essay. And Derby was a visual artist and dancer who had studied African diasporic art and cultural anthropology at Hunter College in New York City. She had been active in the rising Black artist scene that was building there at the time.

Said Derby, "Well, if theater means anything, anywhere, it should certainly mean something here. Why don't we start a theater?" Read that sentence again. It challenges the very meaning of theater. It hangs that meaning on place (rural Mississippi); on audience (rural Black people); and on circumstance (an aggressive and very dangerous challenge to oppression built over centuries). This was *ars gratia populis*: art not for its own sake, the governing principle of the time, but art for the people, a notion that the establishment despised. Furthermore, this was art that would be made in service to radical political struggle; art made by people who were deep in political activism and seen by them as congruent with activism; art that would call the people to assembly and prepare them for action. This is the story I could never tell at the NEA. But it was the best story.

Nor was such activism peculiar to John and his friends at COFO. Political relevance was a defining principal of all the movements listed above. Luis Valdez, for example, started El Teatro Campesino as the agit-prop arm of Cesar Chavez's farmworker movement in California. Amiri Baraka developed his cultural center in Harlem and later in Newark as much for political as artistic reasons. The rights of coal miners and other mountain people never stood outside in the rain at Roadside Theater performances.

Please do not misunderstand me: O'Neal, Moses, and Derby were dead serious about theater, as were Baraka and Valdez and Roadside. These are multiple award-winning playwrights and ensembles, after all. It's just that the FST crew would have thought the project a failure if African Americans in rural Mississippi never gained the right to vote.

So. O'Neal, Derby, and Moses bumped into an obstacle that artist-activists of the 1960s commonly faced: How does one start an organization? What are the elements of a theater? What is it made of? What does it cost and how does one maintain that cost? Where is the money for it and how do we get it? Every year? And what is this 501(c)(3) thing anyway?

Until the 1960s, the field of arts management was nearly vacant. The large established institutions knew management, of course; they knew their way around foundation and government funding; but even they mostly relied upon wealthy individuals who comprised the residue of a Gilded Age patronage system. An artist-led organization like the Martha Graham Dance Company probably could not have qualified for foundation and government grants under today's guidelines. Ms. Graham (a former settlement house dancer, by the way) and her ilk would climb out of a financial hole by taking some rich acquaintances to dinner and pleading for their help.

The three founders of FST started trying out ideas at the drama department at Tougaloo, the historic Black college in Mississippi, but were puzzled about how to make their conception concrete.

So John, Derby, and Moses went to the woodshed for a couple of days. They needed help. They sent a prospectus for the foundation of the Free Southern Theater to Bill Schechner, Moses' friend from the Mississippi Free Press. Bill forwarded it to his brother Richard, a professor at the noted Tulane Drama Department. Richard Schechner invited John, Derby, and Moses over for a weekend at his New Orleans apartment, where they discussed the possibility of housing FST at Tulane and a possible repertoire for the company. They had brought their mission statement with them. It was honest: "While it is true that the theater which we propose would by no means be a solution to the tremendous problems faced by people who suffer the oppressive system in the South, we feel that the theater will add a necessary dimension to the current civil rights movement through its unique value as a means of education." The purpose of the theater was "to use theater as an instrument to stimulate the development of critical and reflective thought among Black people in the South," and "to support the work of civil rights activists."

The FST's received its first contribution in the form of a twelve-dollar check from the poet Langston Hughes. Ensemble members gathered the phone numbers of people who should be contacted in the event that they were arrested. The actors were trained to be activists as well as artists.

The Free Southern Theater was built to be lean and portable. The ensemble traveled in a station wagon donated by Schechner and a used pickup truck. "We're still looking for money to pay for the pickup truck," John would quip years later.

The FST's first production, in 1964, was *Inherit the Wind,* by Jerome Lawrence and (a different) Robert E. Lee, a play about the infamous Scopes trial in a small town in Tennessee in which a schoolteacher was prosecuted for teaching the works of Charles Darwin. Gilbert Moses directed. John O'Neal played Henry Drummond, based on the great defense attorney Clarence Darrow.

In the summer of 1964, Freedom Summer, the Free Southern Theater toured the state of Mississippi, in coordination with COFO. In Greenwood, they performed Martin Duberman's *In White America.* Duberman, a white author from the now-defunct Bauhaus-oriented Black Mountain College, near Asheville, North Carolina, constructed this play with brief vignettes from Black and white historical documents. The play needed no set.

Before the curtain, John told the audience, "You are the actors," and encouraged them to be vocal with their responses to the events on the stage. He wanted the antiphony of the Black church. During the after-play discussion with the audience, an essential aspect of FST shows, a Black man said, "They were telling my story on that stage. Oh, they were telling it. And telling it like it really is." The CORE workers James Chaney, Michael Schwerner, and Andrew Goodman were murdered in Mississippi during that Summer of Freedom tour. The FST added their deaths to the script.

The productions generally were held in school auditoriums and churches. In Mileston, in Holmes County, the play was done outdoors in an unfinished community center—the original had been bombed. Denise Nicholas, who was there, remembers, "Half the roof was there, the posts were there, but the walls were not up yet." The stage abutted cotton fields. "It was incredible and beautiful."

The FST repertoire, of course, featured the plays of Langston Hughes, Lorraine Hansberry, James Baldwin, and Ossie Davis. The nascent Black Arts Movement had not yet reared the great Black playwrights of the 1960s, so the FST took on the task of interpreting the standard repertoire in a manner that related to the audience.

And so, in Ruleville, they mounted Samuel Beckett's masterpiece of the absurd, *Waiting for Godot*. FST, then an interracial company (before the Black Power conception took hold), played *Godot* in whiteface. I initially wondered why John chose such a nihilistic play for a rural Black audience, but the show was very effective. The great Fannie Lou Hamer gave the intermission remarks and told the crowd, "Everyone should pay strict attention to the play because it is due to waiting that the Negro is as far behind as he is." This insightful remark flew in the face of the standard interpretation of the play, where Godot (God) is the symbol of the failure of religion to deliver on its promise. The FST's vocal audiences also immediately recognized the character Pozzo, a wealthy, pompous, and oppressive man. During the after-curtain discussion, FST actors interpreted *Godot* in the context of organization and strategy: how to overcome the Pozzos in their community, and how to stop waiting.

The actors felt that they were playing "the most exciting theater circuit in America."

The Free Southern Theater raised most of its money in New York, so they took *Godot* to the city and mounted it at the New School for

Social Research. Immediately after the performance, the FBI arrested John O'Neal and charged him with being an "unproven conscientious objector," as chickenshit a charge as I've ever heard of. But these were the Vietnam War years, the years of J. Edgar Hoover's covert and illegal Counterintelligence Program (COINTELPRO), and a lot of that kind of thing was going on. John was sentenced to two years of custodial service in Chicago, until he had his sentence transferred to the Bronx.

After his term, John O'Neal returned to New Orleans, where the FST had grown deep roots in the Desire neighborhood (of *Streetcar* fame). Desire became the home base for FST's tours to communities across the rural South over the next fifteen years. But expenses are cumulative. Debt and overhead grew heavy. Funders, ever fickle, moved on to different emphases. It was time to give the Free Southern Theater a dignified death.

Junebug Jabbo Jones

From the enduring DNA of the Free Southern Theater, after its demise in 1980, John O'Neal built Junebug Productions. Junebug was as lean as the original FST and designed to stay that way, focused more on developing original material whose exposed roots dug deep into southern rural culture and beyond. Its salient stock character, the creature of ordeal and survival, was Junebug Jabbo Jones. Mr. Jones actually antedated the FST and, like the FST, originated in SNCC.

Junebug was a common midcentury nickname in the Black community, particularly in the South. For the SNCC workers, Junebug became an archetype—that is, a clever statement or action would elicit the comment "That's something Junebug would say [or do]." John O'Neal eventually added the Jabbo Jones to Junebug, the full name caught on, and the character became a common reference throughout the organization. He was a figment to believe in, a universal repository of wisdom, creativity, and courage.

Jennifer Lawson, a longtime SNCC worker from Fairfield, Alabama, who went on to lead the Corporation for Public Broadcasting, remembers that many SNCC people from northern colleges were intensely interested in rural southern folk culture. She once told me about Worth Long, who gained a national reputation for collecting the music of the churches, streets, and juke joints. "We could be anywhere in Alabama or Mississippi, and Worth would know which churches had the most powerful music, which preachers could send his members into glossolalia, where you could hear the best blues, or which checker clubs you could hear the biggest and best lies in." He also knew how to find the best "outsider" art (a patronizing term), whether pictures, sculpture, installations, or graveyard carvings. SNCC intellectuals like Worth and the prolific and insightful author Charlie Cobb could discuss such art within the context of social and esthetic theory. They took the culture of the rural South as seriously as they took the material conditions that they were endeavoring to change. It was all a part of commitment.

Junebug Jabbo Jones was an archetype, a trickster like Anansi the spider or the Signifying Monkey. He was mother wit in motion, a voice you always stopped and listened to. Junebug Jabbo Jones was the perfect signature for John O'Neal. It was reflexive that he built Junebug Productions from the marrow of this most captivating character.

Junebug Productions

For the next thirty years, John tied Junebug Productions to the work of local southern activists. One example was the Environmental Justice Project of the United Church of Christ (UCC). In the 1980s, the UCC identified that of all communities, African American and other poor neighborhoods were the greatest victims of industrial pollution. They coined the term *environmental racism.* Junebug Productions made drama out of this degradation of the environment and its resultant corruption of the human body, including the high rates of cancer in the Black community.

Cooperative productions would be a salient feature of Junebug Productions from its first season until today. *Junebug/Jack,* written and produced with Roadside Theater, was described as "a thirty-year cultural exchange, performance, playwriting, and national touring collaboration." Junebug Productions has hosted and/or played at Roadside in Whitesburg, Kentucky, the Bronx Puerto Rican theater Pregones, A Travelling Jewish Theatre in San Francisco, and Urban Bush Women in New York.

Often these associations produced joint productions. I once saw a collaborative piece (*Promise of a Love Song*) between Roadside, Junebug, and Pregones produced by the Artist and Community Connection, helmed by the Holdens, wherein the experiences, legends, and music of the three communities flowed seamlessly into one another without damaging the pride of self of any culture. They did not pretend to be the same; nor did they pretend to be different.

A device that John developed, and from which much theater was produced, was the story circle. I have mentioned that after-curtain (if there were curtains) conversations with FST audiences were held from the very beginning, in large part to prepare the rural audiences for the political action (say, voter registration) that SNCC workers were organizing. The practice endured after the SNCC relationship expired. But John noticed that all too often, one loud, long-winded individual, usually a man, dominated the discussion.

As an antidote, John turned to the story circle. Carol Bebelle, the former executive director of the Ashé Cultural Arts Center in New Orleans, said, "He really saw the audience as being the other part of the theater performance. It was, 'We brought something for you. Do you have something to give us?'" Participants were invited to sit in a circle and tell stories. According to O'Neal, story circles were governed by "as few rules as possible and no laws. Well, maybe one law: the law of listening. . . . You don't have to like the story that somebody else tells, but you do have to respect their right to tell it." It was a brilliant piece of civic engagement and a fecund source of material, which Junebug Productions would continue to develop in their work with Roadside.

In Sum

I'm going to end here, though the story is far from complete. It seems irrelevant to list the eighteen plays that John wrote or his numerous residencies and awards. It is his commitment, his originality, his belief in a tangible and culturally rooted theater, which changed at least pieces of the world, that I wanted to write about. He summed himself up:

There are those who view art as . . . all about individuals . . . the prerogative to express their feelings and views. . . . There are others who see art as part of the process of the individual in the context of the community and the community coming to consciousness of itself. In the first case the artist is seen as a symbol of the antagonistic relationship between the individual and society. In the second case the artist symbolizes the individual within the context of a dynamic relationship with a community. Obviously, the latter view is the one that I identify with . . . that gives basis to the notion that the artist is a vehicle for a force greater than himself or herself. . . . It includes the whole spirit of life that we participate in, as well as the whole political, social and economic life.

But I will tell you about one award. At one of the Association of Performing Arts Presenters conferences (please don't make me look up the year), John O'Neal was a featured artist. A "Conversation With . . ." was held, and I was the other conversant. As a means of after-work stress relief, I had started making necklaces and earrings, and before the conversation began, I presented John with the first (and only) Annual A. B. Spellman Award for Elegant Relevance. I handed him a necklace I had made with snake bones and a replica of a medallion that enslaved skilled workers were required to wear when they moved unescorted around Charleston. John's medallion read "carpenter," which I thought apt, as John was such a builder. He was amused. He thought that it was something Junebug Jabbo Jones might wear.

Junebug/Jack (1990)

*Kenneth Raphael, Kim Neal Mays, and John O'Neal
perform* Junebug/Jack *in Whitesburg, Kentucky, 1997.
Photo by Jeff Whetstone.*

Production Information

Junebug/Jack was co-created by Junebug Productions and Roadside Theater, and co-written by John O'Neal, Ron Short, and Donna Porterfield. The play was directed by Dudley Cocke and Steve Kent. Original music was composed by Michael Keck, John O'Neal, and Ron Short. Set and lighting were designed by Ben Mays, and dramaturgs were Dudley Cocke, Steve Kent, and Donna Porterfield. The play and production were a joint project of Junebug Productions of New Orleans, Louisiana, and Roadside Theater of Whitesburg, Kentucky. Theresa Holden was the executive producer.

The original cast included Tommy Bledsoe, Angelyn DeBord, Michael Keck, Kim Neal Mays, John O'Neal, and Ron Short. The first touring cast included Michael Keck, Kim Neal Mays, John O'Neal, Nancy Jeffrey Smith, Ron Short, and Latteta Theresa. Subsequent casts also included Adella Gautier, Shawn Jackson, Carl LeBlanc, and Kenneth Raphael.

Junebug/Jack premiered in Atlanta, Georgia, on October 4, 1990, at the Alternate ROOTS performance festival, toured regionally and nationally until 1999, and was performed in London in 1994.

Characters and Setting

There are six actors—three from Junebug Productions and three from Roadside Theater. All actors play multiple roles and sing, variously accompanied by electric piano, guitar, and fiddle.

Setting: an electric piano, stage right in back of set; a wooden platform, stage left; wooden chairs used in various scenes.

(actors use their own names as they introduce themselves at the beginning of the play; each actor plays multiple characters; the stage is bare, with just a few chairs on each side; chairs and lighting create the set and the environment of the scenes)

(company enters singing)

"HOMEWARD NOW SHALL I JOURNEY"
  Homeward now shall I journey
  Homeward upon the rainbow.
  Homeward now shall I journey
  Homeward upon the rainbow.
  To life unending and beyond it
  Yea homeward now shall I journey.
  To joy unchanging and beyond it
  Yea homeward now shall I journey.

(company repeats the song, then speaks to the audience)

KENNETH Hello! I'm Kenneth Raphael. This is John O'Neal, and this is Adella Gautier. We're from the Junebug Theater Project, which is based in New Orleans, Louisiana.

KIM This is Nancy Jeffrey Smith, that's Ron Short, and I'm Kim Neal. We're a part of the Roadside Theater from the Appalachian Mountains, 'round Kentucky and Virginia.

ADELLA So what you got here is two groups of hardheaded people. Over fifteen years ago, out of concern for what was happening in both of our communities, we decided that whenever we could, we'd get together, share stages, and trade audiences. Junebug would play for Roadside audiences in the mountains of Appalachia, and Roadside would play for Junebug audiences in the Black Belt South. And we have had some fun. Some more fun than others. Out of these efforts to work together we created tonight's production of *Junebug/Jack.*

RON   What we soon found out was that the people in both our communities have a lot in common, especially music and storytelling. Junebug slash Jack—some people spend a lifetime studying those slashes. Junebug is a mythic African American storyteller invented by young people from SNCC, the Student Nonviolent Coordinating Committee, during the civil rights movement. He represents the collective wisdom of struggling Black people. For mountain people, Jack represents the triumph of the human spirit no matter how hard the times get.

NANCY   And tonight we've all come here together to share some of our songs and stories with you.

ADELLA   See, everybody has a story, their own story. I bet you all got some pretty good stories, too. But it seems like it has come to the place where people think their stories aren't worth anything anymore.

KENNETH   Trouble is, seems like some people are always wanting to tell our story for us.

KIM   But we got to tell it ourselves! Otherwise, how we gonna know it's us?

JOHN   And if we don't listen to the stories of others, how we gonna know who they are?

NANCY   Our ancestors came over to this country on big boats with big sheets on 'em, looking for freedom.

KENNETH   Our ancestors came over to this country in the belly of big boats.

NANCY   They got here, and lots of them got kind of wild.

KENNETH   Off the boats in shackles and chains they filed.

NANCY   Some of 'em took to running after game.

KENNETH   Sold off and given a white man's name.

NANCY   Some of 'em died out.

KENNETH   Some of 'em just died.

NANCY   But some of them kept on climbing.

KENNETH   Kept on climbing.

NANCY A little bit further on up into our mountains.

KENNETH Further and further away from their "masters."

(company sings a capella)

"I'VE GOT A HOME SOMEWHERE"

(NANCY *sings*)

> I've got a home somewhere
> I'm leaving today.
> I've got home somewhere

(NANCY *and* KENNETH *sing*)

> I'm leaving today.

(all sing)

> I've got a home somewhere a heartbeat away.

(KENNETH *sings*)

> I want to taste freedom

(NANCY *and* KENNETH *sing*)

> I'm leaving today.
> I want to taste freedom

(all sing)

> I'm leaving today.
> I've got a home somewhere a heartbeat away.

KIM   Of course, now when our people got here, there were people already here. Some say five million people, maybe more. Already been here ten thousand years. They already knowed about this land and how to survive on it, and our people learned from them.

KENNETH   I've got Native American blood on both sides of my family.

RON   Ain't a family in the mountains ain't got some Native American blood in them.

KIM   Wasn't long, though, some of us started acting like they weren't people at all—started calling them names—heathens, savages. Next thing you knowed, we started calling each other names...

KENNETH   Rednecks...

NANCY   Coons...

JOHN   Hillbillies...

RON   Niggers...

(company freezes)

KIM   Wonder why that happened?

RON *(sings)*	**KENNETH** *(sings)*
Which side are you on?	We shall overcome
Which side are you on?	We shall overcome
Which side are you on?	We shall overcome someday.
This is a war we're fighting	Deep in my heart
The battles not yet done	I do believe
We gotta stick together	We shall overcome
Until this war is won.	Someday.

ADELLA   You know sometimes a story or song can start out one place and end up someplace else entirely different. (RON *plays "Dixie" on the fiddle*) Now take "We Shall Overcome." It began as a hymn in the Black church, and was changed to how we know it today during the 1930s tobacco workers' strike in North Carolina.

KIM   "Which Side Are You On?" come out of a coal miners' strike in Harlan County, Kentucky. It was written by Florence Reece.

NANCY Now that tune Ron's playing, you may not recognize it, but that's "Dixie."

ADELLA And some of us have real strong attitudes about it, too.

KIM Dixie started out as an Irish dance tune . . .

KENNETH then it got "borrowed" by African slaves, who used it for their own dances . . .

NANCY then it got "borrowed" by a white musician for his minstrel show . . .

JOHN then the Confederate army took it and used it for their own damnable purposes.

(RON *ends "Dixie";* KENNETH *begins "Jubilo")*

ADELLA Hear that? Change a few notes of "Dixie," and make a brand-new tune—"Jubilo." "Jubilo" is a song that celebrates "Juneteenth," the time the slaves got the news about the Emancipation Proclamation.

JOHN Black folks "borrowed" back the dance tune from all them other people, and used it for their own celebration!

KENNETH Speaking of songs with a complex history, here's one that everybody knows.

"JOHN HENRY"

(KENNETH *sings,* RON *plays banjo)*

> John Henry was just a lil' baby boy
> No bigger than the palm of your hand
> He picked up a hammer and a little piece of steel
> Said, I'm gonna be a steel-drivin' man.

(all sing)

> Lord, Lord.
> Said, I'm gonna be a steel-drivin' man.

(KENNETH *sings*)

> John Henry said to the captain
> A man ain't nothin' but a man
> But before I let that steam drill drive me down
> I'm gonna die with a hammer in my hand.

(*all sing*)

> Lord, Lord.
> Die with a hammer in my hand.

(KENNETH *sings*)

> Now the man that invented that steam drill
> Thought he was doing mighty fine
> John Henry drove steel fourteen feet
> The steam drill only made nine.

(*all sing*)

> Lord, Lord.
> Steam drill only made nine.

(KENNETH *sings*)

> John Henry hammered on the mountain
> His hammer was ringing fire
> He hammered so hard he broke his poor heart
> He lay down his hammer and he died.

(*all sing*)

> Lord, Lord.
> Lay down his hammer and he died.

(KENNETH *sings*)

> Early Monday morning
> When the blue bird begins to sing
> Way up on the mountaintop
> You can hear John Henry's hammer ring.

(all sing)

> Lord, Lord.
> You can hear John Henry's hammer ring.
> You can hear John Henry's hammer ring.
> Lord, Lord.
> You can hear John Henry's hammer ring.

ADELLA   John Henry was a Black man. Course some people say that John Henry was not a real person at all.

KENNETH   They'll tell you he's just a story—a legend.

ADELLA   There's nothing wrong with telling stories and legends.

KENNETH   Of course now, it depends on who's telling the story and why.

ADELLA   Now here's a fella who hails from south Mississippi, and goes by the title of

KENNETH & ADELLA   *(in unison)* Junebug Jabbo Jones!

JOHN   *(as* JUNEBUG*)* I am a storyteller. I say "storyteller" 'stead of liar 'cause there's a heap of difference between a storyteller and a liar. A liar, that's somebody want to cover things over, mainly for his own private benefit. But a storyteller, that's somebody who'll take and UN-cover things so that everybody can get something good out of it. I'm a storyteller, storyteller. Oh, it's a heap of good meanin' to be found in a story if you got the mind to hear, a mind to hear.

I am not the first one to carry the title of "Junebug Jabbo Jones." Neither the onliest to have that name. The very first Junebug started out life as a Negro slave. From the time that he was big enough to see straight, his Maw took one look at him and said, "Lawd, have mercy, this here's going to be one of them bad boogers!" Booger was so bad as a child, he would not take funk from a skunk. Right away his Maw seen it wasn't half a chance for him to make a full-grown man 'fore the white folks to kill him. So when he made seven years old, his mother got together with an auntee, who some people say could work root. They took him down to the river and pretended that he got drowned down there. *(cast begins humming)* They mourned, had a funeral and everything. Wore black clothes for three weeks! But in actual fact, they snuck around the back way, took him down to the Cypress Swamp, turned him over to Crazy Bill to raise. Now Bill was so crazy, he decided to run off and live in the swamp by hisself rather than to live his life as a slave. That's how crazy Bill was. Bill belonged to what they used to call a "good master."

ADELLA   A good what?

JOHN   *(as* JUNEBUG*)* A "good master"! Baptist preacher. He taught Bill how to read and everything. He had every intention to make a preacher out of Bill. Bill had to run off one night during a thunderstorm because that preacher had a fit of rage when Bill showed him where it say in the Bible "It's a sin 'fore God for a man to own a slave or to be a slave." It's in the Book!

That preacher got so mad at what Bill showed him in the Bible, he went to grab hisself a gun. Bill took off running in that thunderstorm. That preacher got Bill lined up dead in his sight. About to pop down on him. Bill stopped, seen where that preacher had the drop on him. Stood stark still. Throwed his hands up in the sky, hollered out something loud in African. Well, don't you know, a bolt of lightning come down out of the cloud, hit the barrel of that gun, sealed it up plum shut, knocked that preacher down on his butt, and turned every hair on his body from jet black to silver white—right on the spot!

Bill came back over there, looked at that preacher all sniveling up in the mud and the rain, smiled kind of sad like to himself, and walked on down in that swamp. And stayed down there, too.

From that night on, anytime you'd pass that white-haired preacher's house, you could see him sitting on the porch with four or five guns beside the one that got sealed shut by that bolt of lightning. He swore, "I'll kill any man that goes down in my swamp to get Bill before I get ready to go for him." But he ain't never went down there. And he ain't never again stood astride a pulpit nor let his shadow fall across the face of an open Bible.

There's lots of people scared to go down in that swamp. Some said they was haints, but they ain't no haints. It was that first Junebug and crazy Bill. That first Junebug stayed down there with Bill from the time he was seven years old 'til he became a full-grown man. Many times they sat up all night long, reading, studying. Since they didn't have to spend all their time working, like all the other slaves had to do. They had plenty of time to think. They studied everything that went on around there. They saw everything inside of thirty or forty miles in every direction. They saw that in spite of the terrible conditions most of the colored people were living up under, in most sections it was more of them than there were white folk. If people could have just seen that, there's no telling what could have happened. Then again, there was a whole bunch of white people that might as well to have been slaves, for all they could get out of life. They seen that between the colored slaves and the poor white people didn't hardly nothin' get done around there unless they were the ones to do it. They seen where people would make little stories and songs to make their days go faster and make their load seen lighter, and they put secret meaning in their stories and songs. But everybody was so busy trying to keep their own heads from getting cracked that they didn't take the time to stand back and look at the big picture that had everybody in it.

Right there, that first Junebug, and old crazy Bill, seen where there was a job that needed to be done. It's a job that needed to be done. They knowed it was a bunch of people that would have killed them for teaching people how to read or spreading news that they did not want spread. They knowed that. "But they was a job needed to be done. And we got to be the ones do it. We got to do it!"

As soon as that first Junebug got big enough to leave out the swamp on his own, he commenced going from plantation to plantation, living by his wit. He'd listen to what people was saying, watch what they were doing, and then, so people could get a better idea what they could do to help change things, make things better, he would tell these over here what these over there been up to. That way, the people that were struggling to make things better would feel support and encouragement. And those who weren't doing all they could, maybe should, would be uncovered, and be made to feel ashamed.

Whenever that first Junebug would find somebody who looked like they might make a pretty good storyteller, he'd help them figure out how they could run away. He'd take them down in the swamp, turn them over to ol' crazy Bill. Bill would teach them how to read, make their figures, everything they needed to know to be good storytellers. Before long, there were a lot of them going around, watching, listening, learning, and telling stories to whosoever wanted to hear. All of them doing it under the title of . . .

ALL Junebug Jabbo Jones!

KENNETH Wait, wait, now that's not his real name. It's just a title of a job that need to be did.

JOHN Yeah, like king.

ADELLA Or queen.

KENNETH Yeah! And they all don't have to be Black.

JOHN And they definitely don't have to be men.

KIM That's right, John. There's lots of women up in the mountains like to tell stories. Good ones, too. There's one about where I come from. You see, there was this family lived way up on the side of the mountain, and they lived like folks lived in that time.

NANCY Which was grubbing out a living . . .

RON and having young'uns to help grub out that living.

NANCY Well, this family sure had . . .

KIM, RON & NANCY *(in unison)* A LOT of young'uns.

RON The first young'un they had they'd named Jack.

KIM A purty good name.

NANCY And after that they just named their young'uns whatever they could.

KIM Well, they got a lot of the names out of the Bible, from Abel to Zebidiah.

RON They went through the Sears, Roebuck catalog—named one Hardware.

KENNETH That's a hard name to live up to!

NANCY Then one morning they woke up and Mommy had another little baby with her.

RON Well, for the life of her she couldn't think up a new name for this little young'un . . .

KIM but they put their heads together and they decided to call him . . .

NANCY, RON & KIM *(in unison)* Jack!

NANCY Reckon by now they'd forgotten that was their first one's name . . .

KIM and when they figgered out what they'd done, it was too late.

RON So they started callin' the oldest boy . . .

NANCY Big Jack . . .

RON and they called the youngest boy . . .

KIM Little Jack.

NANCY Now Little Jack and Big Jack, they really took up with each other.

KIM Little Jack followed Big Jack ever'where he went.

RON But then Big Jack went off to work for this rich feller down the road.

NANCY We'll just call him "King" . . .

JOHN "King Coal" . . .

KIM "King Cotton" . . .

NANCY & RON *(in unison)* always a KING!

KIM Little Jack wanted to go with Big Jack . . .

NANCY *(as* BIG JACK*)* "No, you got to stay home."

KIM Now there was plenty brothers and sisters for him to play with, but Little Jack missed Big Jack something terrible.

RON Then early one morning, Little Jack seen Big Jack coming up the mountain.

KIM Little Jack was just about to give him a big bear hug . . .

RON but they was somethin' bad wrong. Big Jack looked awful. They helped Big Jack back up to the house and put him to bed. But when they took off his shirt, they seen . . .

KIM three big strops of hide missin' out of Big Jack's back!

RON They doctored him best they could, but he kept on getting worser. Finally they knowed that Big Jack was gonna have to have some medicine from the doctor if he was going to get well at all.

KIM Course now they didn't have no money to be going out buyin' medicine with—not to buy nothin' with!

RON Folks just didn't need money much . . .

RON & NANCY *(in unison)* but doctors sure seemed to!

KIM Well, one morning Little Jack come down to breakfast with his best little suit of clean clothes on and a little gunnysack with his workin' overhauls in it.

RON *(as* MOMMY*)* "Just a minute. Just where do you think you're going?"

KIM *(as* LITTLE JACK*)* "I'm headin' off to work for the King so I can get money for Big Jack to have some medicine."

RON *(as* MOMMY*)* "You're too little to be going off to work."

KIM *(as* LITTLE JACK*)* "Well, a man has to do what a man has to do . . . Mommy."

RON And off he went.

NANCY It didn't take Jack long to get down to that King's house. He went up and knocked on the door. King come out and Jack says . . .

KIM *(as* LITTLE JACK*)* "Excuse me, King, but I was wonderin', do you need any work done?"

RON *(as* KING*)* "Well, you're a mighty scrawny little rooster, but I reckon I can get my money's worth out of you. Pays a dollar a day. You interested?"

KIM Jack was right in for that.

RON *(as* KING*)* "Oh, by the way, there's one more little deal. Anybody works for me goes by my rules. Whichever one of us makes the other one mad first gets to throw that one down and take three strops of hide out of his back. See now, if I make you mad, I get three strips of hide out of your back, and I don't have to pay you nothin'."

KIM *(as* LITTLE JACK*)* "And if I make you mad, King, I get three strops of hide and my wages?"

RON *(as* KING*)* "Yeah, if you make me mad. I'll tell you what Jack. I'll throw in a bushel of gold, 'cause you can't make me mad. I'm the King."

KIM *(as* LITTLE JACK*)* "Well, King, we'll see about that."

NANCY Jack had come a long way and was awful hungry, but he was awful proud, too, and his Mommy had raised him not to beg, so he says . . .

KIM *(as* LITTLE JACK*)* "Reckon I better wash up before I eat supper."

RON *(as* KING*)* "Eat! Boy, you ain't done nothin' to deserve no supper!"

KIM *(as* LITTLE JACK*)* "But . . ."

RON *(as* KING*)* "Now, that don't make you mad, does it?"

KIM *(as* LITTLE JACK*)* "No, I ain't mad. Just hungry."

RON *(as* KING*)* "Oh, good. Now you see that corncrib out there?"

KIM *(as* LITTLE JACK*)* "That's a corncrib?"

RON *(as* KING*)* "No. That's your hotel for tonight!"

KIM *(as* LITTLE JACK*)* "Now just a minute, King. I come all the way from Mommy's house, you won't give me nothin' to eat, and now you expect me to sleep THERE?"

RON *(as* KING*)* "Um . . . Yeah. It don't make you mad, now does it? You don't mind, do you?"

KIM *(as* LITTLE JACK*)* "Shucks no. I don't mind."

RON *(as* KING*)* "Oh, good. Now get. You got a hard day's work ahead of you."

NANCY Next morning, Jack went up to the King's house bright and early, but the King met him outside.

KIM *(as* LITTLE JACK*)* "Uhhh, King. Something smells good! What's for breakfast? I could eat a hog."

RON (*as* KING) "Breakfast? You just don't get it, do you, boy? You ain't done nothin' to earn no breakfast."

KIM (*as* LITTLE JACK) "Look here, King, I'm gettin' awful hungry!"

RON (*as* KING) "Why Jack, you ain't gettin' mad, are you?"

KIM (*as* LITTLE JACK) "No, I ain't mad! It's just low blood sugar."

NANCY The King took Jack out to the barn. Showed him his fine flock of sheep and says . . .

RON (*as* KING) "Jack, take my sheep up to the high meadow. Don't you lose a one of 'em!"

KIM So Jack took them sheep way up in a high meadow. But he was so weak that he just laid down underneath a shade tree. Felt like his stomach was playing tag with his backbone. When this purty little lamb went skippin' by, sayin' . . .

NANCY (*as* LAMB) "Ba, Ba, Ba."

KIM But Jack was so hungry, it sounded like that little sheep was sayin' . . .

NANCY (*as* LAMB) "LUNCH, LUNCH, LUNCH."

KIM Jack banged him on the head, built him up a fire, and had him a fine lunch of roast mutton.

NANCY That evening, he took the rest of the sheep back to the King's house. There was the King, counting the sheep.

RON (*as* KING) "996, 997, 998, 999 . . . Jack, where's my little prize lamb with the black ears?" (*to audience member*) "Excuse me, have you seen my lamb?"

KIM (*as* LITTLE JACK) "Well, King, you hadn't given me nothin' to eat and I was mighty hungry, so I eat him."

RON (*as* KING) "You eat my lamb? That was my little prize lamb I was raising for breeding."

KIM (*as* LITTLE JACK) "Yeah, King, it was a good lamb alright, tasted mighty good."

RON (*as* KING) "You good-for-nothin' . . ."

KIM (*as* LITTLE JACK) "Why King, are you mad?"

RON (*as* KING, *trying to hold back anger*) "No . . . I ain't mad."

NANCY   But that night, the King fed Jack a real good supper . . .

KIM   and fed him a good breakfast the next morning, too.

NANCY   Took Jack out to the field, where he had a fine horse hitched up to a plow.

RON   *(as* KING*)* "Can you plow? I want you to plow up this patch for me. I aim to put in some turnips."

KIM   *(as* LITTLE JACK*)* "Of course I can plow." So Jack gitty-up'd that horse, and set out plowing these long, straight furrows.

NANCY   The King watched him, got satisfied Jack knew what he was doing, went on back to the house.

KIM   About that time, this old woman come down the road, riding this old rickety horse.

NANCY   *(as* WOMAN*)* "Rickety, rackety, humpity, bumpity."

KIM   You could hear its bones clanking together, it was that poor. *(as* LITTLE JACK*)* "Hey, good morning, Moms. That sure is a mighty fine horse you got there."

NANCY   *(as* WOMAN*)* "Why Jack, you ought not make fun of a old woman who's got the best she has!"

KIM   *(as* LITTLE JACK*)* "No, I think that is a fine horse. Why, I bet the King wishes he had one like that. I don't suppose you'd be willin' to swap horses with me?"

NANCY   *(as* WOMAN*)* "It's a deal!" *(off she gallops)*

KIM   Jack hitched that old rickety horse to the harness and set in to plowin' that field . . .

KIM & NANCY   *(in unison)* just as crooked as a dog's hind leg.

NANCY   When the King come back . . .

RON   *(as* KING*)* "Hey, Jack, how you doin'? Wait a minute! Where's my horse?"

KIM   *(as* LITTLE JACK*)* "Right here, King. That big ol' fat horse eats too much, so I swapped him for this'un. This'un won't eat too much."

RON   *(as* KING*)* "You swapped my fine workhorse for this bag of bones?"

KIM   *(as* LITTLE JACK*)* "King, you sound mad. You ain't mad, are you?"

RON *(as* KING*)* "No, I ain't mad. It's just that low blood sugar, I reckon."

NANCY But the King decided he wasn't gonna let Jack near no more of his animals. The next morning, Jack was to pick apples.

RON *(as* KING*)* "You do know how to pick apples, don't you?"

KIM *(as* LITTLE JACK*)* "Sure do."

RON *(as* KING*)* "Well get to it, boy."

NANCY The King sent Jack up to the orchard with some bushel baskets and a ladder . . .

KIM but Jack snuck back down to the house and got a big double-bit ax . . .

NANCY and went to cutting down them big fine apple trees.

KIM *(as* LITTLE JACK*)* "TIMBER!"

NANCY And then he picked the apples off the limbs once they was down on the ground.

KIM *(as* LITTLE JACK*)* "It's the modern way!"

NANCY Then the King came out.

RON *(as* KING*)* "Hey! What in the devil are you doin'?"

KIM *(as* LITTLE JACK*)* "Pickin' apples."

RON *(as* KING*)* "Boy, you're gonna ruin me, you big dumb hillbilly. Don't you know NOTHIN'? You don't chop down the trees. This is how you pick apples."

NANCY And he took the ladder and set it up against one of the trees, climbed up the ladder, and went to picking apples and putting them in his sack.

KIM *(as* LITTLE JACK*)* "Well, that's one way of doin' it alright. But what if somebody was to come up to you and do this . . ."

NANCY and he yanked that ladder out from under the King. The King just had time to latch his arm over a limb.

RON *(as* KING*)* "Jack, you let me down. Put that ladder up here this minute!"

KIM *(as* LITTLE JACK*)* "I don't like the way you been treatin' me, and I don't like the way you treated my brother. But I'll put the ladder back if you'll get your wife, the Queen, to make me a big deep-dish apple pie."

RON *(as* KING*)* "Okay, okay. Go tell her I said to fix you one."

KIM So Jack went running down to the house, knocked on the door, and the Queen come out.

NANCY *(as* QUEEN*)* "Yeah, what do you want?"

KIM *(as* LITTLE JACK*)* "Queen, the King said for you to give me a great big kiss."

NANCY *(as* QUEEN*)* "In your dreams, sonny boy."

KIM *(as* LITTLE JACK*)* "Hey, King, she says she won't do it!"

NANCY *(as* QUEEN*)* "Am I supposed to do what he says?"

RON (as KING) "Yes, yes, give him what he wants right now!"

*(*LITTLE JACK *gives* QUEEN *a long kiss)*

RON *(*KING *gets out of tree; runs up to house)* "Now you're gonna get it! I'm gonna bust your head wide open!"

KIM *(as* LITTLE JACK*)* "What's the matter, King? Are you mad?"

RON *(as* KING*)* "You're durn right I'm mad! I'm gonna . . . uh-oh . . ."

KIM Jack throwed him down right then and there . . .

NANCY cut three big strops of hide off of the King's back . . .

KIM collected a bushel of gold, and went on back home. He went in to where Big Jack was and seen he was bad off. Family was sure he wouldn't make it 'til morning. But Jack took them three strops of hide out of his pocket, washed 'em off real good, and laid 'em out on Big Jack's back. They fit just fine.

NANCY Next morning, Big Jack was up eating breakfast. It wasn't long 'til he was up and working around the place, feelin' fine.

KIM And to this day . . .

NANCY Big Jack . . .

KIM Little Jack . . .

NANCY all their children . . .

KIM grandchildren . . .

NANCY and greats . . .

KIM & NANCY *(in unison)* are doing well.

KIM   And folks still say that that entire family has got . . .

KIM & NANCY *(in unison)* royal blood in their veins!

"DOWN ON THE FARM"

(RON *sings*)

Cornmeal bread and cornmeal gravy
They'll make you fat
But they won't make you lazy
Talkin' 'bout the good ol' things down on the farm.
Black-eyed peas and collard greens
They'll fill you up but they'll
Keep you clean
Talkin' 'bout the good ol' things down on the farm.

CHORUS *(all sing)*
London, England, Paris, France
Ain't none of them places stand a chance
Talkin' 'bout the good ol' things down on the farm.
Don't care 'bout Betty Crocker's Gold Medal
Ain't nothin' no better than my Mama's iron kettle
Talkin' 'bout the good ol' things down on the farm.

(ADELLA *sings*)

Rabbit stew and squirrel gravy
Drive you wild
But it won't make you crazy
Talkin' 'bout the good ol' things down on the farm.
Fried squash

(RON)

Fried 'maters

(JOHN)

Fried corn

(all)

Fried taters
Talkin' 'bout the good ol' things down on the farm.

CHORUS *(all sing)*

(NANCY *sings*)

Apple pie and stawberry jam
Make me sweet as I am
Talkin' 'bout the good ol' things down on the farm.
That ol' wild turkey and wild corn
Make you glad that you was born
Talkin 'bout the good ol' things down on the farm.

CHORUS *(all sing)*

KENNETH I live in the big city now, but I grew up in the country. My grandfather had over eight hundred acres of good bottomland in south Mississippi. We still own a nice little farm down the Dog Leg Branch off from the twin oak trees on the New Caledonia Road. New Caledonia Road? That's the road that runs from Seven Waters over to Four Corners. Four Corners? Now Four Corners ain't too far from Magnolia, which is a big little town sits on old State Highway 27, about nine miles south and a little bit west from Macomb, Mississippi. *(to cast)* I don't believe they know where that's at. *(to audience)* You know where Jackson, Mississippi's at? *(drawing an imaginary map)* Well, take that for New Orleans. And this is Jackson. My home is right there. Right there. Part of Pike County.

RON Pike County? Pike County is in Kentucky.

KENNETH Well, this Pike County has got to be different. You see there used to be plenty of people up in there. It was almost enough Black people for us to start our own little town, but now my brother's the only one still got a working farm up there. *(*JOHN *reminds him to say more about* CHARLIE MOFFETT*)* Oh, Charlie Moffett is still on the county registry, but he's working two jobs in Macomb to pay rent on the land he was born on, in a house his daddy built with his own hands.

RON It's the same way in Pike County, Kentucky. There was a time, when if you had the right to a piece of land and was willing to work it, you could make a living off that land. But then it got to the place where you couldn't do a thing if you didn't have money. When they brought money into the mountains "to help us out," the people started moving out, and they took our land away.

JOHN There was a time when Black people gave blood, sweat, and tears to get forty acres and a mule. But now Black-owned land is being lost at the rate of about 42,000 acres a month. It's hard to see it when land is being lost, 'cause the land don't go nowhere.

NANCY *(as* OLDER WOMAN*)* Now it's not that hard to see in the mountains, 'cause they'll cart off a whole mountain in the back of one of them big dump trucks to make a strip mine. Still and all, when people lose their land *(cast drifts off one by one to city)*, they sort of drift off a few at a time, so you don't really notice what's happening 'til they been gone for a while.

I don't rightly know when things started to change. They never did for me really. Saw all my young'uns marry off and leave, but even 'fore then it wasn't the same. I never liked the idea of my children moving off, nor going to work in the coal mines, but they wasn't nothing I could do about it. Once they knowed about them things they didn't have, it was too late.

We worked hard, and I can rightly say my young'uns never went cold or hungry for lack of something to wear or food to eat. We never had much, but we always had plenty. It's not what you've got, it's what you're satisfied with.

I know children are different from their parents, but they's things that they want that I don't even know about, or care to. But I guess that's the whole thing. You know what you know. It's kinda like that little story about Adam and Eve. It wasn't the apple that got 'em into trouble, it was what they knowed after they eat it. And they ain't no turning back from that.

KIM When we went to Dayton, I was so excited about living in a big city. I was gonna get new clothes and go to the movies. I was gonna play with kids that wasn't my cousins. But I never did fit in. I tried, but I was just too different. Mommy said it wasn't me different, it was them, but it didn't seem that way to me. I got to thinking there was something wrong with me. You know it seemed to me like going off to Dayton was like headin' for the promised land, but I ended up in the wilderness, believing in nothing or nobody.

"CITIES OF GOLD"

(RON *sings*)

> Tell me where do you come from
> Tell me where will you go
> To the mountains around you
> Or the Cities of Gold.

> **CHORUS** *(all sing)*
> Cities of Gold, Cities of Gold
> Oh so lonely and so cold
> You can lose your very soul
> Living in Cities of Gold.

(RON *sings*)

> Now the people, they said to Pharoah
> You better let our children go
> 'Cause we're tired of livin' our lives
> So you can build your Cities of Gold.

CHORUS (*all sing*)

ADELLA   (*as* YOUNG WOMAN) Everybody in my family could sing. Our dog, Red Rover, you could give him a harmony part and he'd hold it. No matter how tired Momma was when she got in from work—she cleaned houses for people—she'd be in the kitchen, humming to the pots and pans. After dinner my brother, my sister, my daddy would start harmonizing on some old church song, and it'd be no telling how long before we went to bed—two or three o'clock in the morning. But we were not the only ones could sing. We had ourselves a powerful singing preacher at our church. Reverend Sister Gary didn't just sing, she knew how to bring the music out in people. Our whole church would be rocking. Music tied our family together, united the members of the church and community. Music was everywhere—revivals, funerals, weddings, a big rally of some sort, marching with my daddy in the movement. And we'd be there singing.

One Sunday morning, my cousin Sheila paid us a surprise visit at our church. Now before Sheila moved to Dayton, she was the best singer around. When she walked in, she looked like a picture straight out of *Ebony* magazine. She took her seat in the choir. A hush fell over the church. Reverend Sister Gary said, "Sheila, sing us a song." Sheila stood up, cleared her throat, and cut loose. Child, three people asked to be accepted into membership before Sheila finished singing.

Sheila told me, "Girlfriend, the only reason you won't get what you want in the city is if you don't have the gumption to stoop down and pick it up!" The very next day I said, "Mama, I'm going to Dayton, where Sheila live."

Mama said, "Dayton or no Dayton, you finish high school, 'cause I ain't gonna take care of your children in my old age!"

NANCY "Amen!"

ADELLA *(as* YOUNG WOMAN; *to audience)* See how they all stick together! Well, I finished high school, mainly for her, but the ink wasn't dry on my diploma before I was on the bus, heading for Dayton. When I got to Dayton, Sheila looked like a different person at the Greyhound station. Her face was all pinchy and she was coughing all the time. This white man said, "You got your claim check?" and I said, "Yassuh, right here." Sheila said, "Girl, you better leave all that country stuff at home. You don't have to be sniffing up to no white folk here in Dayton. Here man, just give her her stuff!"

Sheila got me a job in the plant where she was working. I worked side by side with this white woman, Kim. Me and Kim hit it off pretty good. Both our hands going nonstop to keep the assembly line moving. We hit production and then some. One day we found out we knew some of the same old church songs. We just started singing together while we worked, during break, after lunch, just for the heck of it. Course she sang like white folks sing, and I sing like Black folks, but we ended up laughing our heads off about how it sounded when we put that together. And we found out that neither one of us was scared to speak up for our rights. We didn't take no stuff off of nobody. That's how we became union leaders.

We seen that of all the promotions that year, not one had been a woman, a Black, or a Mexican. So we spoke up about it. Sheila coughed and said, "You better leave that crazy white girl alone. Ain't neither one of y'all got no sense." But before long a Black man got promoted.

The mess really didn't start 'til we seen all the supervisors and the managers walking around wearing these white protective masks over their faces when they were on the floor. Well, we didn't have masks on the line. We were the ones working right in the pollution, and we didn't rate to be protected. Me and Kim said, "Hey, what's up with that?"

We went to the boss and he listened. "Uh-huh. Uh-huh. You fired. And you know you fired, gal."

Me and Kim, we lost our jobs. Sheila kept her job, and kept on working there. But Sheila never sang no more. *(pause)* Sheila died before she was thirty-two.

JOHN   I was eighteen years old before I got set to leave home. A lot a fellers hung around back home until they was big enough . . .

NANCY   or bad enough . . .

JOHN   to go in the army. But the first one I ever remember to outright leave home with no intention to return was my friend Philip Anthony "Po" Tatum.

KENNETH   *(as* PO, *spoken word)*
   I'm going to the City
   Where the women's really pretty
   And they tell me that the money fall like rain
   I'm tired of picking cotton
   Mississippi's gotten rotten
   I'm gonna pack my bags and jump the quickest northbound
      train!

JOHN   'Fore long, everybody was singing Po's song.

KENNETH   *(as* PO*)*
   I'm going to Chicago, baby
   Heading for the City
   I'm going to Chicago, baby

(all)

   Heading for the City
   Chica-Chica-Chica-chica-Chica Chicago
   Chica-Chica-Chica-chica-Chica Chicago
   Chica-Chica-Chica-chica-Chica Chicago
   I'm going to catch a northbound train!

ADELLA   *(yells)* "ZUDIO!"

"ZUDIO"   *(all recite and dance the "Zudio")*
   Here come Zudio, Zudio, Zudio

Here come Zudio all night long
Step back, Sally, Sally, Sally
Step back, Sally, all night long
Walking down the alley, alley, alley
Walking down the alley all night long
Looking down the alley, what did I see?
A BIG FAT man from Tennessee

JOHN (RON *becomes fat man;* JOHN *yells)* "There he is!"

(all)

I betcha five dollars that you can't do this
To the front, to the back, to the side, side, side
You lean way back, then Ball the Jack
You lean way back, you get a HUMP on you back
You lean way back, you get a HUMP on you back
You lean way back, you get a HUMP on you back
You do the CAMEL WALK
You do the CAMEL WALK
You do the CAMEL WALK!

JOHN By the time Po got to the city, there were lots of games like Zudio to be played, but Po already had his mind set on other kinds of games, games where there was money to be made. He started playing with the boys from the big time—ended up in jail. Years later, I found Po in Chicago. One of the things he was trying to do to straighten himself out, get his life back together, was making a garden in the city and organizing others to do the same. By that time he had changed his tune.

KENNETH *(recites as* PO*)*
I got a garden in the city
My okra's really pretty
I ain't had no greens that tastes so good since I was home
I had to put aside my shopping
That grocery bill left me rocking
I had to leave that doggone grocery store alone

I'm living off my garden, baby
Garden in the city
I'm living off my garden, baby
Garden in the city
Diga-diga, diga-diga, diga Chicago
Diga-diga, diga-diga, diga Chicago
Diga-diga, diga-diga, diga Chicago
Trying to make myself a brand-new home

JOHN   Yeah, my man Po, seemed like the system just got the best of him. He went out in a blaze of glory, trying to change the whole thing all by himself.

(keyboard plays)

"SPOKEN WORD" (JOHN *and* KENNETH)
You can't judge a book by looking at the cover
You can read my letter
But I bet you can't read my mind
If you want to get down, down, down
You got to spend some time
I want to walk with you, I want to talk with you
I wanna, wanna, wanna, wanna rap with you

(KENNETH *as* PO)

When you grow up in the country
Things are hard
Times are tough

(JOHN)

You growing your own food but it never seems enough
You too smart for the country

(KENNETH *as* PO)

> You got to get away

(JOHN)

> You move to the city
> Got to be a better way

(KENNETH *as* PO)

> So you move to the city
> Put the country stuff behind

(JOHN)

> But when you hit the city
> It starts to messing with your mind
> You struggle and you scramble
> Try to do the best you can

(KENNETH *as* PO)

> You think you working for a living
> Hell, you working for the Man
> People stacked like chickens on the way to meet the
>   slaughter
> Flopping all around the ground like fishes out of water

(JOHN *and* KENNETH *as* PO)

> Blind man on the corner
> Holding up a sign
> "No More Water, Y'all, the Fire Next Time."

RON *(as* SOLDIER*)* "AT EASE!"

KIM *(skipping rope)*

    G.I. Haircut

    G.I. Shoes

    G.I. Hardtack

    G.I. Blues

    G.I. Love You

    G.I. Do

    G.I. Hope you love me too.

RON *(as soldier)* "Attention!"

JOHN *(as soldier)*

    You had a good home but you left, your right

    Sound off 1, 2

    Sound off 3, 4

    Bring it on down

    1, 2, 3, 4

    1, 2 . . . 3, 4.

"BROTHER TO BROTHER"

*(*KIM *sings)*

    Now that you've gone away

    The sunlit days don't seem as warm as they used to be.

    Since you're not here with me

    What once was clear now seems all lost in a mystery.

*(*NANCY *and* KENNETH *echo* KIM*)*

    Brother, are you safe and well

    There's so much to tell

    I need me someone just to talk to.

    Brother, won't you come home soon

    No one else can cheer me

    No one else can chase away the gloom.

(KIM *sings*)

Brother, why'd you go away
Brother, what's a hero
Leaving home makes no sense to me.
Daddy said you had to go away
Tell me what you're fighting for
Brother, help me understand your wars!
Brother, help me understand your wars!

(KIM *sings*)

Stay safe, my brother
Hurry home, my brother
There's someone here who needs you
And loves you.

(*spoken*)

"Brother, what's a hero?
And why do you have to go away to be one?"

NANCY   *(as a mother)* When my son Luke graduated from high school, it looked like there was no way for him to go on to college like some boys was able to do. He'd been talking to them recruiters that was always at the school telling the boys about all them military benefits. *(guitar begins playing the theme of "Vietnam")* Oh, he didn't want to wait, he wanted us to sign for him so he could go on in.

His daddy wouldn't do it, and I didn't want to. But he was getting into trouble pretty regular at the time, and he told us that it looked like he could go off to the service or go off to jail. Well, his daddy said at least he'd be alive in jail, and he still wouldn't sign. Luke kept at me and kept at me, and he got into more and more trouble all the time. Finally, I signed. *(music stops)* He had just turned eighteen when he finished basic and shipped out to Vietnam. He ended up a machine gunner in the Eighth

Marines, and was pretty much in constant combat for a year. We got letters from him. Sometimes the handwriting was so big and scrawled that he would only get about five words on a page.

(guitar plays)

KENNETH When I was in Nam I laid up on a ridge, looking down at this village. There was women, children, pigs—I felt like I was home. I told the captain, "The only way we gonna win this war is to kill every man, woman, and child in the country."

(music stops)

JOHN *(as captain)* "Well, if that's the way they want it."

(guitar plays intro to "Vietnam")

"VIETNAM"

(KENNETH *sings*)

> I went walking one morning
> The Devil took me by the hand
> Said "Come on let me show you 'round my little place
> I call it Vietnam.
> Ain't so much to look at
> Just a quaint little jungle land
> But before I'm through, it'll mean the world to you
> You won't forget Vietnam."

> **CHORUS** *(cast joins* KENNETH*)*
> Vietnam, where the sweetest flower died on the vine.
> Vietnam, it'll steal your heart, steal your mind.

So come all you space-age children
You ain't never gonna understand.
If you want to see real living and dying
Come over to Vietnam.

Pride is the first thing that leaves you
Fear is the last thing to run
And you can't see too well when you're staring into hell
Down the barrel of a gun.

CHORUS *(cast joins* KENNETH*)*

(Tag)

Momma, don't you know me, I'm the boy next door
Can I come home?
Momma, don't you know me, I'm the boy next door
Can I come home?
I went walking one morning
The Devil grabbed me by the hand
Said "Come on, let me show you 'round my little place
I call it Vietnam.
Ain't so much to look at,
Just a quaint little jungle land.
But before I'm through, it'll mean the world to you
You won't forget Vietnam
You won't forget Vietnam
You won't forget Vietnam
You won't forget Vietnam."

NANCY *(as* MOTHER*)* That year my boy was in the war, I lost forty pounds, and my hair turned completely gray. Seemed like the time would never pass. The days just stood still. It was like mothers all over this country was holdin' their breath, waiting.

When he come home, I thanked God that he was safe, and that we could go back to being a family. But it wasn't long until I could see things was different. Oh, he never missed a family gathering, but he always come late and left early. And when he got married, he never even told me about it until it was over and done. I tried everything I knowed to bring my family back together, but things was never the same after that.

JOHN *(as soldier)* When the Korean War ended in '53, I shipped home, and like a lot of my buddies I joined the Reserves. Two years later, we read in the papers where Emmett Till had been lynched in Money, Mississippi. *(organ plays "We Shall Overcome")* Some of my Reserve buddies couldn't understand why I was so upset about that one child being killed in Mississippi, when we'd seen hundreds of Korean children die during the war. I tried to explain it—what it was. After we fought all over the world in the name of freedom, then to have a fourteen-year-old boy to be lynched in the "land of the free and the home of the brave" was just too much. That's when I knew it was time for me to quit the Army for good. I was fighting on the wrong side in the wrong war. *(music fades)*

RON I had this buddy. We was both medics. We wasn't in the fighting like them Marine and Army guys. We picked up the pieces after the fighting was over. Day after day the same thing, trying to save the pieces of what was left. Pretty soon you're looking for anything to talk about instead of that, and somebody to talk to.

One day I heard him say he was from Washington, D.C. Most of my people had been forced to move out of the mountains back in the fifties, looking for work. They ended up around northern Virginia. I told him about my people and everything, and we started talking. He told me his family was from North Carolina, but he was raised in D.C.

After that we just sort of started hanging out together. Both of us loved Muddy Waters. A lot of friendships been started on less than that. We was friends.

In April that year, I got rotated back to the States. It was hard to explain, but somehow I kinda hated to leave. I remember thinking I must be going crazy, not wanting to go home.

I went home on a thirty-day leave. But I swear to God, in a week I couldn't stand it. I'd watch that television and see them pictures, and it was like I'd keep looking, trying to see myself. They didn't even remind me of me.

I ended up in Greeneville, Mississippi, on temporary duty. My orders got screwed up, and three months later I was still there. Then I'll be damned if my buddy from Nam didn't show up. Oh man, we had a party! It was just like old times.

One night we decided we was gonna go into Greeneville, but there was a big football game that night and the town was deserted. Somehow or another we decided to go to a movie. I don't even remember what was playing. We got our tickets and went on in, got some popcorn and Pepsi, started to go into the movie, when this woman says, "Hey, you can't go in there!"

I said, "Excuse me?"

"Now you know better than that. He can't go in there. He has to set up there," and she pointed to the stairs going up to the balcony.

I said, "We're in the service. Me and him is together, ma'am."

She said, "I don't care."

He never said nothing the whole time. Then he just turned around and walked out. I just stood there holding a box of popcorn and a Pepsi.

We got a cab back to the base. But it never was the same after that. *(music begins)* I ended up in Illinois. He went to California. I never saw him again.

"THE ONLY WAR THAT'S FAIR TO FIGHT"

(KENNETH *sings*)

The only war that's fair to fight is the

(all sing)

War to end oppression.

(KENNETH *sings*)

The only war that's fair to fight is the

(*all sing*)

War to win your freedom.

(KENNETH *sings*)

The only war that's fair to fight is the

(*all sing*)

War you fight to win your human rights.

(KENNETH *sings*)

The only war that's fair to fight is the

(*all sing*)

War to end oppression.

"TREE OF LIFE"

(RON *sings*)

Ain't you got a right

(*cast sings*)

Ain't you got a right

(RON *sings*)

Ain't you got a right

(cast sings)

Ain't you got a right

*(*RON *sings)*

Ain't you got a right

(cast sings)

Ain't you got a right

(all sing)

To the tree of life.

(chorus repeats; piano joins)

*(*ADELLA *sings)*

You may be Black

(cast sings)

Ain't you got a right

*(*ADELLA *sings)*

You may be white

(cast sings)

Ain't you got a right

(ADELLA *sings*)

> Ain't you got a right

(*cast sings*)

> Ain't you got a right

(*all sing*)

> To the tree of life.

(NANCY *sings*)

> Gonna tell my brother

(*cast sings*)

> Ain't you got a right

(NANCY *sings*)

> Gonna tell my sister

(*cast sings*)

> Ain't you got a right

(NANCY *sings*)

> Ain't you got a right

(*cast sings*)

Ain't you got a right

(all sing)

To the tree of life.

(KIM *sings*)

You may be young

(cast sings)

Ain't you got a right

(KIM *sings*)

You may be old

(cast sings)

Ain't you got a right

(KIM *sings*)

Ain't you got a right

(cast sings)

Ain't you got a right

(all sing)

To the tree of life.

(JOHN *sings*)

> You may be hungry

(*cast sings*)

> Ain't you got a right

(JOHN *sings*)

> You may be cold

(*cast sings*)

> Ain't you got a right

(JOHN *sings*)

> Ain't you got a right

(*cast sings*)

> Ain't you got a right

(*all sing*)

> To the tree of life.

"WHAT DID THEY DO" *(upbeat; lively spoken word with music)*

> ***CHORUS*** *(all)*
>> What did they do with what they took from you
>> What did they do with mine
>> No use complaining what they took from you
>> They been stealing from us all a long time

(JOHN)

Ancient red man chief stands looking in grief
The damage done to Mother Earth
Lots of blood been shed through the years
No pain can equal its worth
Can't measure the sorrow of the buffalo people
Used to dwell from shore to shore
When the Pilgrims began it was the red man's land
Before they were forced to go
Those that are left, land lost few
Forced onto reservations
Trail of Tears, battles lost and won
Endless treaty manipulations
Fighting in the courts
They been using the system
Organizing a plan
Standing with their brothers and sisters
Winning back their land

(KENNETH)

A lot of Black people all over the world
Still fighting a terrible fight
Thinking 'bout the past but looking to the future
Beginning to see the light
History has proven that it's unacceptable
To keep a people down
Pain and suffering all those years
Shackled and whipped to the ground
Families disrupted, where is the justice
Millions gone to slave ship sea
With faith intact they broke their backs
Three hundred years of labor for free
Now the only request after giving their best

Was for forty acres and a mule
Asking and waiting and asking again
Still treated like a fool
It's been a long time since 1865
Some changes are hard to see
But freedom for you and freedom for me
Everybody in equality

CHORUS *(all)*

(RON)

For over one hundred years people in the mountains
Lived in peace and harmony
Helping one another, living on the land
They knowed what it meant to be free
Then some men from the banks, church and government
Men from the industry
Took a look at the mountains, put their heads together
Said with disbelief
There's something wrong with this picture here
And there's gonna be hell to pay
You need money to spend, credit cards and bills
To live the American way
You can't buy my pride
You can't sell my hope
You can't steal my identity
And when the air we breathe is sold a breath at a time
Hillbillies will still be free

(NANCY)

Things have been bad for
The women of the world
Since the dawn of time began

From the Garden of Eden
To the streets at night
They blame us for original sin

(KIM)

Our bodies exploited for greedy gains
A way to sell and promote
We hear "Relax and enjoy it, baby"
Regardless of what we want

(ADELLA)

We want equal pay for equal work
Respect for our right to choose
If I want to be a mother, a wife, or a lawyer
We can do anything we want to do

(NANCY)

The Earth is our mother
The only place that our children will know
Let's save the land, give them a future
A place where we all can grow

(NANCY, ADELLA, *and* KIM)

Changes for me mean changes for you
Let's help each other all we can
There's a job to be done
A war to be won
And we don't need a gun or a man

CHORUS *(all)*

(ADELLA)

> The forces of evil tryin' to keep us down
> Are getting stronger every day
> Between Iran Contra and Desert Storm who knows
> How much we gotta pay
> Millions and millions of welfare dollars
> Have been spent since '33
> Won't equal what they stole from the Savings and Loan
> But here's the real tragedy

(KIM)

> We got our people on the streets

(NANCY)

> Crack in our schools

(RON)

> Children living with AIDS

(ADELLA)

> And our national debt going through the roof

(JOHN)

> Lord help you if you tell them you're gay

(ADELLA)

> 'Cause they'll try their best to take what's left
> Hold on to your self-pride

(All)

'Cause greed is the villain and whoever is a-willing
Can join in the militant line
Don't be upset if we seem to forget
And left out your personal beef
We're all sisters and brothers if we're doing unto others
We all share the grief
The battle's not easy, the path's rough and greasy
It's gonna take a little more time
It might take some effort
But you and me together
Can get to work 'til we find

CHORUS *(all)*

(two cast members go to audience on either side of the theater, and get audience on their feet to join repetitions of the chorus)

(left side of audience) WHAT DID THEY DO
(right side of audience) UH-HUH, UH-HUH
(left side of audience) WHAT DID THEY DO
(both sides of audience) OH YEAH

(at appropriate time, cast members return to the stage and end with)

LET'S GET IT ALL BACK THIS TIME!

——— **END** ———

Promise Then and Now

Arnaldo J. López

I. Then

First we hear an Irish hand drum, the musician's silhouette gradually revealed under a single spotlight. A Creole tambourine and a Latin conga follow in sequence, each instrument and its player similarly showcased under bright light for a long moment. The rhythmic eruption of a drum set then rolls into crescendo. Before long, keyboards, horns, bass, and guitars join in, and the lights go up on a six-piece band in full swing, reveling in the mix of African American, Puerto Rican, and Appalachian themes.

"It is a singular moment of fusion," said multi-instrumentalist composer and musical director Ricardo Pons, "and a subtle contest of musical styles."

This formidable sound is the opening moment of *Promise of a Love Song*. It is a unique meeting of peoples and cultures: the mostly Puerto Rican Pregones Theater, based in the South Bronx and known for musical adaptations of Spanish Caribbean literature; Junebug Productions, a social change-oriented African American theater company from New Orleans; and Roadside Theater, champions of the Appalachian folk traditions of rural eastern Kentucky. These three professional theater companies came together to form the Exchange Project, a five-year creative experiment, of which *Promise* was the capstone.

I first met the artists of the Exchange Project in 1997. I was in New York for graduate school, following twelve formative years in Pennsylvania, where I studied on scholarship at a liberal arts college and worked as a graphic designer. Two years later, I traveled with Pregones, Junebug, and Roadside during their period of feverish creative activity and heated negotiations leading up to the show's premiere at the New Orleans Contemporary Arts Center. That experience, in all its struggle and beauty, cemented my faith in the theater, and my feeling that I had a place in it. Shortly afterward, I joined the staff of Pregones, where I have worked ever since.

True to the identities of its artists, *Promise*'s original score incorporates jazz, rhythm and blues, bolero, salsa, jig, and lullaby. "We meant to preserve the root of each music in relation to each of the stories being told onstage, not just find a happy blend, which is often dishonest," noted Donald Harrison, Jr., a renowned jazz artist and composer who worked on the show.

Pregones, Junebug, and Roadside were acquainted with one another's work long before the idea for the Exchange Project surfaced. Each ensemble had been making and performing works for more than twenty years. They had met one another through participation in Alternate ROOTS, the southern stalwart of community-based arts. They had seen one another's work and had collaborated in various ways, including through the nationwide multicultural American Festival Project. Though their styles varied greatly, there was a commonality in their approach to theater that kept drawing them together. They shared a passion and deep respect for popular artistic expressions, a history in post-1960s social activism and performance, and a mission to create works to honor and bolster Puerto Rican, African American, and Appalachian cultural identities—in opposition to the crass cultural stereotyping and social and economic marginalization they encountered in mainstream consumer culture and the exploitative economy that fueled it.

Pregones first invited Roadside to perform for its home audience in the South Bronx in 1994. They billed the Appalachian artists' first weeklong residency as a festive gathering of storytellers, actors, poets, and musicians, featuring performances of Roadside's *Mountain Tales and Music* and a rousing *controversia*, or music jam, between local and guest musicians. Everyone in attendance left clamoring for more. Later that year, Roadside invited Pregones and Junebug to Whitesburg, Kentucky, for a new round of performances and conviviality. The convergence of African American artists from New Orleans and Puerto Rican artists from New York in the coal-filled mountains of central Appalachia was rife with energy and significance from the get-go.

The three groups continued trading songs and stories and visiting one another's stages. They traveled in round-robin fashion, playing, surveying, discussing, and making plans. Once they got the knack for exchange, they started considering a more involved collaboration. In 1997, they came together to announce the co-creation of a new theater work, and the Exchange Project was officially under way. Financial support came from the National Endowment for the Arts, the National Performance Network, the Lila Wallace–Reader's Digest Arts Partners Program, and the James S. and James L. Knight Foundation, as well as from the New York State Council for the Arts, New York City Department of Cultural Affairs, and Arts Council of New Orleans. The project was co-commissioned by the Cincinnati Arts Association/Aronoff Center for the Arts; the Columbia Festival for the Arts, in Maryland; the Flynn Theater for the Performing Arts, in Vermont; and both the Wagon Train Project and the Lied Center for Performing Arts, in Nebraska. As this list of sponsors suggests, right from the start this was a collaboration intended to reach audiences of mixed racial, social, and economic makeup.

In addition to carving out room for experimental collaboration, the Exchange Project scheduled local residencies designed to advance arts-related debate and cultivate a multicultural audience. Related activities included artist-led workshops, story circles, concerts, lecture-demonstrations, and Q and A sessions. In New Orleans, where *Promise of a Love Song* had its first public presentation in October 1999, the five-week schedule at the Ashé Cultural Arts Center and the New Orleans Contemporary Arts Center included open rehearsals, where neighbors could witness the thrilling and often contentious play-creation project firsthand.

The play itself is made up of three different stories, one from each company. Pregones's artistic director, Rosalba Rolón, also codirector and dramaturg of *Promise of a Love Song,* envisioned the three companies onstage simultaneously, telling their stories one bit at a time. In that way, the stories would gently tangle up with one another. Rolón wanted to explore how a formalized proximity would affect the three seemingly self-contained but parallel narratives.

"You put three different peoples onstage and something's bound to happen," agreed Ron Short, old-time music master, playwright, and a key member of Roadside's ensemble. "We rarely see Appalachian, Puerto Rican, and African American people together. They may be in the same room, but we don't actually see or hear their detailed cultural and ethnic histories, the subtleties of their language, their very own sense of humor and geography, the important truths they have to tell each other."

One immediate challenge was the choice of subject matter. Rolón recalls: "As we grew to know each other's histories, it became evident that heartache and centuries of social injustices were a common thread and we were at risk of creating a piece that would amount to a collection of tragedies and melodrama. One day, over dinner in Whitesburg, I shared a dream I had the night before. I dreamt that the play was about love and lovers. We laughed, then looked at each other. And we began to think 'what if'. . ."

The script ended up interweaving three love stories. In Roadside's "Charming Billy," an elderly mother cares for a son living with developmental disability, both shaped by the hardships and blessings of rural life in Appalachia. Pregones's "Silent Dancing," adapted from a story by Judith Ortiz Cofer, juxtaposes a young woman's memories of growing up Puerto Rican and her father's plight as an immigrant in New York. Junebug's "Star-Crossed Lovers" tells of two Black activists building a family in the bosom of the civil rights movement. Together, the three stories grapple with intersecting and distinctly American embodiments of race, culture, language, geography, and oppression. Each has its own accent, color, and historical context. Each also triggers certain narrative expectations in the audience. To watch the show is to have those expectations constantly readjusted.

The jagged musical jam at the top of the play sets the scene for a storytelling contest between the three companies. Each story has its own charms and gravitas to offer, but not all at once. The actors must vie for attention from the public, and from one another, one scene at a time. They will gradually fall into an also jagged rhythm marked by sequential shifts from one voice, one place, one culture to the next. This formal assemblage mirrors the actual experience of intercultural work between Junebug, Roadside, and Pregones, fueled at irregular intervals by both conflict and love.

The artists of the Exchange Project were not shy about acknowledging that conflict was a generative force in the making of *Promise of a Love Song*. In my conversations with them leading up to and following the New Orleans premiere, there also lingered a bittersweet frustration in knowing that the play succeeded in embodying an aesthetic expression of conflict and love, tempered by each other, yet the real-life intercultural and intracultural dramas that shape and misshape the lives of working-class people in the United States remained imperviously in place.

I am convinced that it is the music, and a closely related counterpoint musicality in writing and structure, that lend *Promise* its most distinctive and lasting qualities. The riddles of culture and the struggles of working people that the creators chose to portray find their finest correspondence in the common groove that animates the popular music of Black New Orleans, Appalachia, and the Puerto Rican Bronx.

"The three stories resonate onstage much like the three styles of music do," said Steve Kent, longtime collaborator with Junebug and Roadside, who shared director's credit with Rolón. "The story lines may be teased apart, but the real challenge is something different. The stories develop through gesture and choreography and sound. Sometimes the action in one story underscores the action in another. Sometimes it contradicts it."

Similarly, when the lights burst or fade from one scene to the next, when one line of music trails over another, what is staged is not the singularity of neatly framed vignettes, but how they spill over and press up to one another. On this musical theater stage, as so often in our lives, we are a lot closer to our neighbors than we think.

II. Now

Paradoxically, looking back at *Promise,* what I remember most is looking ahead. Multicultural coalitions based in shared struggle and outward-facing collaboration are always looking toward what's next. "I know we won't see the new humane society we're trying to make," John O'Neal once said. "It's going to take some more work after we get through."

Twenty years later, the relationships that led to *Promise of a Love Song* enjoy a rich afterlife. The show seeded several more creative projects between Junebug, Roadside, and Pregones. And inspired by their work together, each theater company also launched other intercultural initiatives, discovering rich value in working with unlikely partners. Prior to the Exchange Project there was no name or ready-made template for this kind of work.

For this publication, I reached out to the artists involved in the premiere and two-year national tour of *Promise.* I asked them to share their thoughts about the production and their experience being involved in it, twenty years on. As a starting point, I offered five prompts in the form of questions—in some ways similar to a story circle. The overwhelming response was one of affirmation. Yes, *Promise* was a meaningful and important experience for me. Yes, I cherish my time with fellow artists of the Exchange Project and learned enduring lessons. Yes, the production was prescient in the ways it approached intersectional oppression and the theater's formidable capacity to help us see it and address it.

Recurring observations touch on pride of culture and place, the joys and challenges of collective theater making, the disarming quality of stories firmly rooted in real lives, and the transformative potential of empathy. Love and conflict and music are again underscored as part and parcel of *Promise of a Love Song*—its ultimate gift.

Question 1

What place or activity stands out foremost in your mind as representative of your experience with Promise, *and why?*

ALVAN COLÓN LESPIER, Pregones Associate Artistic Director: The process stands out. It demonstrated that cross- and intercultural work can be carried out without compromise. Each company was firmly rooted in the cultures that they grew and worked in; each saw in art and specifically in theater making a means to explore our histories and envision a better future for all.

JORGE B. MERCED, Pregones Associate Artistic Director, *Promise* Cast Member: My principal takeaway from this experience is a clear understanding of how essential it was for us to have artmaking at the center of the Exchange. I don't believe we could have established the trust or given each other the license we needed during the creative process had it not been for the shared goal of making a work of art together. That common goal enabled us to step out from behind the armor of cultural representation, and to truly appreciate each other in close proximity.

ROSALBA ROLÓN, Pregones Artistic Director, *Promise* Codirector and Dramaturg: What stands out is being able to develop the play in each of our communities, our cities and towns. Spending quality time together, both artistic and social, building a family that loved, fought, was at times happy and at times angry, all those things that emerge as we create across cultures.

NICOLE McCLENDON, *Promise* Stage Manager: I had a childhood dream of writing a play that could effect world peace, and when I saw *Promise* onstage, I started to believe in that dream again. New Orleans was the first of many places where we gathered to break bread with one another. The work that took place in rehearsal kept going in conversations over shared meals peppered with laughter, and as we shared those meals, we also shared our personal selves with one another. I was constantly amazed to see such deep friendships between people who might not have come together were it not for *Promise*.

Question 2

Is there a story line or character that has stayed fresh in your memory, and why? What do you recall best about the interplay between the three stories and their characters onstage?

CAROL BEBELLE, Ashé Cultural Arts Center Director: I remember the soft whisper that called the character of Mother to speak up, the red ribbon and the dancing that animated the story of the family from El Barrio, and the poetry and music of the civil rights couple. I remember particularly the poem "Promise of a Love Song."

SOLDANELA RIVERA, Pregones Actor, *Promise* Cast Member: My entire involvement with the Exchange Project is unforgettable, with many lessons that still linger. There was one performance at the Contemporary Arts Center in New Orleans that stands out as a transcendental experience. Mother is singing to Billy onstage. I was listening to the scene unfold from behind the scrim, when suddenly I felt weightless and outside of time, with an enormous feeling of compassion for the lives of all of us onstage. At that moment, I felt the triumph of the project—there was common ground, acceptance, union, and respect among the players and among our characters. Billy's vulnerability belonged to all of us, we were him, we were his mother, fighting hard for dignity. It was but a few seconds that seemed to last a long time, and still do.

RON SHORT, Roadside Ensemble Lead, *Promise* Writer, Composer, Cast Member: These characters are people that no one had ever met before; they are people that most people will never meet, and they had never been in the audience's mind until we tipped the scale by presenting these stories. Though the stories were very different, ultimately it was three stories about the longing for human dignity, and a transcendence over the world of prejudice.

Question 3

What is your musical memory of the show as a whole? Are there one or more aspects of the play's sonic tapestry and/or its development that stand out for you?

ALVAN COLÓN LESPIER: Even though we had all seen and heard each company's work before, that had occurred in independent sittings. This time around, the artists and musicians were exploring ways to come together in a fashion that did not dilute or appropriate each other's styles, approaches, or inspirations.

TROI BECHET, Junebug Actor, *Promise* Cast Member: The through line of love and music is the brilliance of this play. Though the stories could stand easily on their own, it is in their interweaving that a beautiful portrait of humanity is orchestrated. From the plaintive melody of the Appalachian folk song, to the pulsing rhythms of salsa, to the cathartic strains of the blues, *Promise* offered a moving sound track. Independently, the many styles of music offered listeners a lyrical entrée into the cultures represented. The real magic for me was the opening overture. Its melding of the many cultural styles was a musical metaphor for the intertwining love stories.

RON SHORT: Music may be the hardest part of cultural collaboration. Musical memory, styles, nuances reside at the deepest part of our cultural identity. Attempting to be a part of someone else's musical identity is a perilous journey and calls for both courage and sensitivity, and it is the hardest performance task to accomplish. Nobody wants to look foolish in their attempts to take on such a daunting task and nobody wants to abandon the safety of their own identity. Yet that is exactly what our collaboration was about.

RICK SEBASTIAN, Junebug Musician, *Promise* Band Member: We all had a lot of creative input in arranging the music that Donald brought to the show, and these are always my favorite projects. We had challenges playing some of the Latin music, and the Latin musicians in the group had challenges playing some of the jazz and blues that Donald and I were very comfortable with. One of the challenges was to get the music to flow with the show, and we succeeded greatly, in my opinion.

ROSALBA ROLÓN: *Promise* taught me that music is not a universal language. The language of music, with its individual nuance per culture, needs to be learned, needs to grow inside of you. While the music for each of the stories was very beautiful and very grounded, it was the moments in which musicians played together, mixing sounds, rhythms, and perspectives, that stand out most.

Question 4

On occasions when you thought the performance was at its best, who, do you remember, was watching, and what do you think contributed to the success of the show?

THERESA HOLDEN, *Promise* Executive Producer: I often think about what happened at the Lied Center for Performing Arts in Lincoln, Nebraska. In one of the postshow story circles I led, a white woman said the story of the African American family resonated most clearly with her own life story. Then a white man said the Puerto Rican father's tale of struggle to take care of his family was his own father's story, "to a tee." And on it went. The power of family stories from people of completely different races and places crossed over that divide and rang true to this primarily white audience. That experience in that theater that night did more to prove our shared humanity across race and place than any lecture or history lesson.

NICOLE McCLENDON: I was not alone in wondering how all the nice stoic midwestern folks would react to *Promise*. From almost the first note there was movement in the seats. Not of people changing seats or walking about, but from folks moving to the music.

RON SHORT: During a question-and-answer period in Alabama (don't remember the city) a young Black woman stood up and said, "I found myself feeling sympathy for the white people in Billy's story. Then I caught myself; that surprised me. . . . I don't think I had ever felt sorry for white people, but their story touched me, and I had to catch my breath and think about everything I had thought before. They were feeling things that I had felt."

Question 5

In hindsight, what do you remember as the most daring and/or difficult aspects of creative experience, and why? What would you say is the great promise in Promise?

CAROL BEBELLE: The big promise of *Promise* is the capacity it has to engender compassion and empathy.

JOSÉ JOAQUÍN GARCÍA, Pregones Actor, *Promise* Cast Member: I think a daring aspect of the piece is that all three stories were of equal importance and that in some deep way this challenged white supremacy culture and the underlying illusion of what race is here in the United States. The overcoming of obstacles in each of the stories, for me, was the gathering point for the audiences. No matter where one came from, there was something in this musical to root for. If staged today, it would pack a wallop.

THERESA HOLDEN: As is often the case, this play and these artists' voices were powerful then, and in some ways ahead of their time. The image of these three cultures sharing a stage, shining a light on the shared humanity of all people, no matter their race, or where they came from, was powerful then and seems even more needed today. Artists have always been our soothsayers, pointing out through song, poetry, and stories what the current issues and problems are and how we might see a different way to approach them.

NICOLE McCLENDON: Looking back on *Promise,* I think one of the many aspects that were both daring and difficult about it was learning how to talk to each other. I know that sounds simple, but sometimes the hardest thing for strangers to do is greet one another. Not only did the artists and collaborators dare to say hello but they also took the time to learn how to greet each other in a language or dialect different than their own.

RICK SEBASTIAN: I think that the most daring and difficult thing about *Promise* is that it attempts to bring to light different perspectives of inequity in America, which is even more apparent during the present time. Being old enough to remember the civil rights movement, I know that we have come a long way in dealing with racial injustice and inequality, but there is still so much to do and a slew of different problems that need a light shone on them. Only then will we be able to confront those issues. *Promise* made many people uncomfortable because it exposed glaring problems that are often swept under the rug regarding race relations.

DONNA PORTERFIELD, Roadside Managing Director: The creative experience may have appeared daring—and it certainly was difficult—but it couldn't have come about without the years each company spent drilling down into its own local life and exploring its own local history and traditions. Plus, the three ensembles had spent years visiting and performing in each other's communities as a way to see firsthand what was held in common and what was not held in common. The result was a performance in which audience members of each culture felt their traditions and realities affirmed, which, in turn, allowed them to embrace the commonalities and accept the unresolved historical tensions that set them apart. No one was a victim, and that was the great promise in *Promise.*

Promise of a Love Song (1999)

Performance of Promise of a Love Song, *1999. Actors: Kim Neal Mays, Ron Short, Soldanela Rivera, Jorge Merced, John O'Neal, and Adella Gautier; musicians: Desmar Guevara, Ricky Sebastian, Waldo Chávez, Donald Harrison, Jr. Photo by Jose J. Garcia II.*

Production Information

Promise of a Love Song was a project of Junebug Productions, Pregones Theater, Roadside Theater, and the Exchange Project. The musical drama was written by John O'Neal, Rosalba Rolón, and Ron Short, with music by Donald Harrison, Jr., Desmar Guevara, Ricardo Pons, and Ron Short. The play was directed by Steve Kent and Rosalba Rolón. Music director was Ricardo Pons. Set and lighting were designed by Douglas D. Smith, and costumes were designed by Theresa Holden. The executive producer was Theresa Holden.

The original cast included Kim Neal Mays as Mother, Adella Gautier as Donna, Donald Harrison, Jr., as the son of Donna and Nelson, Jorge Merced as Father, John O'Neal as Nelson, Soldanela Rivera as Angela, and Ron Short as Billy. The original band included Waldo Chávez, Desmar Guevara, Donald Harrison, Jr., Ricardo Pons, and Ricky Sebastian.

Promise of a Love Song premiered in 1999 at the Ashé Cultural Arts Center and the Contemporary Arts Center in New Orleans, Louisiana; the University of Virginia's College at Wise, Virginia; and Hostos Center for the Arts and Culture in New York, New York. The production toured nationally until 2002.

Characters and Setting

The characters are members of three families, plus the band musicians. The Appalachian family includes Billy and his mother. The African American family includes Nelson, Donna, and their son, Donald. The Puerto Rican American family includes Angela and her father.

Setting: There are three distinct playing areas: a simple rural Appalachian house, a New York tenement, and a New Orleans shotgun house. Each area has a scrim and full curtain in front of it, which can be opened and closed as needed. The scrim depicts the locale for each playing area. Both the scrim and the curtain create various effects, such as silhouettes and lighting patterns. There is a fourth playing area for the band, which is set upstage of the rest. There is a scrim for the band area, which can be opened or closed, but no curtain. The band area is as significant as the other three, as characters emerge from there to take on roles, and characters from the other three playing areas interact with the band throughout the piece. Once the actors and musicians enter the stage, they remain onstage for the entirety of the play's action, moving seamlessly from one playing area to another. Lights, music, and other effects determine the focus of the action. Place and time vary as each story is told.

ACT 1

Scene 1

(all performers enter; musicians go to the bandstand and tune their instruments; each male actor moves to his respective playing area—a rural Appalachian house, a New York tenement, and a New Orleans shotgun house; as banjo softly plays "Greenwood Side'eo," the actors in New York and New Orleans open their curtains; the rural Appalachian curtain remains closed)

Scene 2

(the soft sound of cymbals fill the stage; MOTHER *opens scrim 1 curtain; cast whispers in sequence as* MOTHER *puts on an apron)*

ALL   *(in a whisper)* Mother . . . Madre.

Scene 3

(lights come up on MOTHER *in Appalachian house; two other women, one in New York house and one in New Orleans house, look on and listen to* MOTHER; *she sings "Greenwood Side'eo")*

MOTHER
> There was a lady lived in York
> All alee and lonely
> Fell in love with her father's clerk
> Down by the Greenwood side'eo.
> She loved him up, she loved him down
> All alee and lonely
> Loved him 'til he filled her arms
> Down by the Greenwood side'eo.

MOTHER   Aunt Mary Holyfield, who was my doctor that brought me into this world, taught me that song. She brought many a young'un into this world, so I reckon somehow or other that song about them poor little babies that never had a chance stuck with her. It stuck with me. I thought it was the saddest tragic story ever.

MOTHER   *(sings)*

> She bent her back against an oak
> All alee and lonely
> First it bent and then it broke
> Down by the Greenwood side'eo.

MOTHER   When I was a young girl, I'd sing it and cry for her. Mommy didn't like me singin' it, said it wasn't proper in the first place and it caused me to be too melancholy in the second. And she said that come from having too much time to think. *(lights fade)*

Scene 4

*(*DONNA*'s "Paris Theme" is heard; lights come up on New Orleans shotgun house as* DONNA *puts on a stole, swirls around, and sings)*

DONNA

> The nighttime seemed as bright as day
> With all the lights on Old Broadway
> I was overwhelmed the first time that I went there.
> But New York's charms were swept away
> When first I went to Paris
> The elegant way
> The Champs-Élysées
> Embraced the small café that lived there.

DONNA   In '64 I won a scholarship to study law at the Sorbonne. Oh what a time to be a student in Paris! I met many of the great Black artists and intellectuals in exile—Richard Wright, Josephine Baker, Louis Armstrong *(pause for trumpet's arpeggio)*, and lots of others. *(sits)* One evening, I was invited to participate in a salon that James Baldwin, "Jimmy," was hosting in his home. He was even more eloquent in real life than he was in print. He spoke of how "the Movement" had changed his life. He needed the relative freedom from American racism that he found in Europe in order to write. At the same time, as a "native son," he had to take part in the struggle for justice in America.

He also spoke of the passion of a young Movement leader in Louisiana named Nelson Hardiman. Like Baldwin, Hardiman was a brilliant high school dropout, who Jimmy thought was cut from the same cloth as Malcom X and Nelson Mandela.

(DONNA's "Paris Theme" ends; background kalimba music begins as lights come up on NELSON standing on a platform behind the New Orleans scrim; audience sees through the scrim and into the past; DONNA sits in front of scrim in the present)

NELSON   *(over background music)* When I was a kid, every time the circus came to town, me and my best buddy would be the first ones there to help set up. If they paid us fifty cents, they'd pay the white kids a dollar, but we didn't care. We'd have been there if they hadn't paid a penny. We weren't just chasing a dream, we were learning things.

They'd use the elephants to do the heavy lifting. They'd hitch the elephant to the big poles that hold the tents up, then tell him to "pull!" A single elephant could raise a whole tent by himself. When they didn't need that elephant anymore, they'd take him off to the side and tie him up to a little stake in the ground with a rope. And the elephant would stay there! That elephant, who could lift a whole huge tent by himself, wouldn't pull a little stake up from the ground because he was afraid to be free!

DONNA   Baldwin's stories of the passionate young hero were magnetic to me.

NELSON   *(following a rhythmic beat, NELSON's voice fades as he delivers the following lines, emphasizing the word* fear *and fading the rest of the* *line, retreating, while* DONNA *speaks over his fading voice)* FEAR keeps us from calling a spade a spade.

DONNA   He was so bold.

NELSON   FEAR keeps us riding on the back of the bus!

DONNA   Fearless.

NELSON   If these white people were truly committed to the struggle for justice, they'd be fighting against racism in the white community. I tell them to take on the Klan, the White Citizens' Councils. Hell, let them take on their own mamas.

DONNA   He was willing to talk about white people out loud in public the way most of us would only whisper in private. It was so liberating. *(lights on* NELSON *fade; kalimba music ends;* DONNA's *"Paris Theme" resumes, bringing her back to the present)* I admit, I'd been tempted by the romantic challenge of living the lush life on the Left Bank of Paris among the Afro literati. But after that evening at Jimmy's house, I knew. A seed had been planted in me that would become my life's work. I knew I had to go back home. *(*DONNA's *"Paris Theme" ends; lights fade)*

Scene 5

(musicians play "Toda una vida"; lights come up on New York tenement house; FATHER *sings two verses of "Toda una vida" behind the scrim while* ANGELA *opens a trunk in front of the scrim; she finds letters represented by several yards of paper rolled and tied with a red ribbon)*

FATHER   *(sings)*
　　Toda una vida
　　Estaría contigo
　　No me importa en qué forma
　　Ni cómo ni dónde
　　Pero junto a ti.
　　Toda una vida

Te estaría esperando
Te estaría adorando
Como vivo mi vida
Que la vivo por ti.

(spot comes up on ANGELA*)*

ANGELA   *(reading letters)* "Dear Gramma, I don't know what Mami has told you about our new life in the States. Has she told you about our apartment? It is tiny, in a huge apartment building that had once housed Jewish families, they tell me. It has just been turned into a tenement by us. *(pause)* Hey, it is almost 1960, Puerto Ricans have arrived! So here we are in el building. Papi's doing well with his job in the Brooklyn Navy Shipyard and all."

(to audience) My father. My father died a long time ago. (FATHER's *shadow can be seen behind scrim;* ANGELA *continues reading)* He says that with myself and my brother, the military was the only option away from the sugarcane fields in the island. *(she chooses another letter)*

FATHER & ANGELA   "Querido hermano, las cosas por acá están bien." (FATHER's *voice fades as* ANGELA *continues reading)*

ANGELA   "Sé que no querías que me enlistara en el Navy, pero no había otra opción fuera de las centrales de caña, y con una esposa y dos niños. Todavía estoy asignado al Brooklyn Yard." *(puts* FATHER's *letter down; picks another letter; reads on)* "I like it here, I guess. But everything is gray, the streets, the building, even the coat that Papi bought for me. Anyway, I'll write again soon. Your favorite granddaughter, Angela."

(band plays "El Recuerdo," which means "remembrance"—a bolero; FATHER *comes in front of scrim and faces Angela; they move together as if dancing; looking sideways at the outside world;* FATHER *stands on the trunk and pulls a long strand of rolled red ribbon from his pocket and throws it over*

ANGELA's *shoulder; she catches it and ties up her hair with one end of the ribbon as* FATHER *makes a tie from the other end; he throws the strand of letters over her shoulder, which she catches; she reads them silently as* FATHER *reads them out loud)*

FATHER "I continue to look for a larger apartment. Not that we are uncomfortable or anything, but I do want what's best for my family. The children are small for now, but they will need more space eventually. In the meantime, I have given strict orders to my wife to keep the doors locked, *(bolero ends abruptly;* FATHER *looks sideways, as if looking out a window)* the noise down, ourselves to ourselves."

("Greenwood Side'eo" plays as lights fade on New York tenement and come up on rural Appalachian house)

Scene 6

(BILLY *appears behind Appalachian scrim; banjo music is heard; the band plays an overlapping Latin rhythm; Latin rhythm drops out as* BILLY *takes his place by* MOTHER, *sitting; follow spot comes up on* BILLY *playing the notes to "Greenwood Side'eo" on banjo;* FATHER *sits in New York tenement house, writing letters;* NELSON *sits in New Orleans shotgun house, reading)*

MOTHER Mommy was fifteen when she married my daddy. He was eighteen or nineteen. Had eight children all told. I was the fourth. Started out on a piece of land belonged to Daddy's daddy. I remember Mommy telling how she got water out of the head of the Pound River. It starts as a spring and gets bigger as it goes along. *(pause;* BILLY's *and* MOTHER's *hands move together in a gesture that follows the flow of the water;* FATHER *and* NELSON *make subtle sounds, breathing, turning pages, handling paper)*

MOTHER I was born on Big Branch in 1910. Growed up down there. Went to school at Osborne's Gap, finished up the seventh grade.

(sings)

> She bent her back against a thorn
> All alee and lonely.
> There she had two wee babes born
> Down by the Greenwood side'eo.

I married Wesley Mullins in 1926. I was sixteen years old. I had my first baby in 1927. We named him Henry. In 1929 I had a baby girl. We named her Hetty. In 1931 I had another little boy, and his name was Lewis James. In 1933 Billy was born. *(lights up on* ANGELA *staring out from New York tenement; "Greenwood Side'eo" ends)* Then I had a daughter in 1935, and her name was Lilly. In 1937 I had another little boy, and his name was Clovis.

BILLY   Bud. *(*BILLY *gets up and leaves;* ANGELA *drops curtain)*

MOTHER   Bud. We called him Bud. I don't know what got into us. In 1940 I had another girl. Her name was April. We ran out of names and began using months. In 1944 we had another baby. We named him Dwight David. *(*BILLY *sits near* MOTHER*)* Mommy had eight and I had eight. Every household had about that many. Some had more. They didn't pay no 'tention to it, you just raised 'em and that was it. When we first married, we lived all over the place. Last sixty years, though, I've settled down some. My husband's gone now these past thirty years, and the children all married off and left me—except Billy.

BILLY   *(sings)*
> Can she bake a cherry pie, Billy Boy, Billy Boy?
> Can she bake a cherry pie, Charming Billy?

(continues singing softly as MOTHER *speaks)*

MOTHER   Billy was eleven when he started takin' fits. Then he started in on that singin'—the same thing over and over—sometimes it didn't make any sense at all.

BILLY   *(sings)*
St. Luke, Mark and John
Hold ol' Pete while I get on.

MOTHER   Over and over 'til he'd just freeze and fall and start shakin' all over. They got worse and worse.

BILLY   *(sings louder and louder)*
Billy Boy, Billy Boy.
I'm a wise boy, but some boys
Are silly.

MOTHER   Then he'd just set for a long time and stare out.

BILLY   (BILLY *gets up)* This'n here don't remember. That'n says she does, so I guess she does. When it comes to it, if you can believe one, that's good. Them ain't got nothin' to do with it. Us ain't got nothin' to do with it. This'n and that'n, that's all they is.

MOTHER   He went to school 'til the seventh grade. He was always smart. But the seizures got so bad, and he got to where he hurt people. Pinch and hit. Not cruel, I don't think, just like that singing, (BILLY *sings softly)* not able to help it. And they said he couldn't go no more.

BILLY   *(sings)*
Home, home on the range
Where the deer and the antelope play
Where seldom is heard a discouragin' word
A discouragin' word, discouragin' word.

BILLY   Why, I asked that'n? WHY? The rest of 'em goes. That'n says this'n is goin' to a special school. So we go.

(lights fade on BILLY *and* MOTHER *and the Appalachian house)*

Scene 7

(band plays "Sincerely Yours/Funkily Yours"; lights come up on DONNA *in the New Orleans shotgun house)*

DONNA *(takes briefcase; walks from behind scrim to downstage)* I had to fight against smile-in-your-face racists every step of the way, but I finished Yale Law with honors in 1968 and took a job with the NAACP Legal Defense Fund.

NELSON *(lights come up on* NELSON *behind the scrim)* I stand with Mrs. Fannie Lou Hamer, who was kicked off her job as a timekeeper on a Mississippi plantation because she had the gall to go register to vote. Her byword was, "I'm sick and tired of being sick and tired!"

DONNA The papers always showed him in some angry pose, fist clenched above his head, with his mouth stretched wide. Distorted. But the more the media tried to make us hate him, the more the people loved him.

NELSON Brother Kwame Ture's right. "The Black man's got no business going to fight the yellow man to defend a country that the white man stole from the red man in the first place." *(music ends)*

DONNA But when he came out for armed struggle in South Africa and the PLO and against Israel and the war in Vietnam, the white power structure decided he'd gone too far. Though he hadn't even been charged with anything, Hardiman was dragged from his bed in the dead of night, beaten and held for weeks at the notorious Angola State Prison. Reluctantly, the NAACP national office agreed that we should take the case.

NELSON They put this headstrong young woman, fresh out of law school, on my case. They said that's the best they could do.

DONNA I did all my legal homework, but I couldn't get a judge to hear the case until I got national network news to cover James Baldwin speaking about the Hardiman affair at a rally in New York.

NELSON As it turned out, it was the best they could do.

DONNA The very next day, they let Hardiman out on bond. The road was muddy and rough, but we got there.

NELSON When the guards came to get me out of my cell, I didn't know if they intended to lynch me or cut me loose.

DONNA I knew what he looked like. I'd seen him on TV and in the papers. But I was not prepared for what happened when he stepped into the room.

(NELSON *comes downstage from behind scrim; band plays soft arrangement of "Sincerely Yours")*

NELSON *(avoiding* DONNA's *gaze)* I felt the woman before I saw her.

DONNA My heart began to pound. I felt faint. I wondered if the others noticed.

NELSON What was this I was feeling?

DONNA He acknowledged the group, then slowly he turned and he took me into a private place deep inside himself. *(facing each other)*

NELSON When we looked at each other, I felt like she had seen me—I mean, really seen me. It was like she knew things that I'd have told her before I had to say a word.

DONNA In the backseat of the car, we sat together silently all the way back to New Orleans. *(they sit)*

NELSON We went to my office. Worked late into the night.

DONNA He went to the place where he'd been staying.

NELSON I packed a few clean clothes.

DONNA We went to my new apartment.

NELSON & DONNA *(in unison)* We've been together ever since.

(they look at each other and kiss; lights fade on New Orleans shotgun house as DONNA *hugs* NELSON; *he delivers a verse of "If I Could Promise You a Love Song")*

NELSON
> If I could promise you a love song
> I'd take a meter soft and sweet and curve the words
> Until they meet the place your smile leaves off.
> I'd make a song that smiles the way you do
> If I could promise you a love song.

(music ends; lights down on New Orleans shotgun house; lights up on New York tenement; a young ANGELA, *with ponytails, lovingly teases* FATHER, *who is seated on the trunk, writing letters; in Appalachian house,* MOTHER *playfully tries a new vest on* BILLY; *all three playing areas are now illuminated by bright pools of light)*

Scene 8

(band—keyboard and congas; a young ANGELA *dances and speaks; she writes to her grandmother;* BILLY *sits, cleaning his banjo;* NELSON *writes)*

ANGELA   *(reciting her letter)* "Dear Gramma, mark today's date as my first spanking in the United States, as a result of playing tunes on the pipes in my room to see if there would be an answer. There are these pipes, you see, they are called heater pipes. They bang and rattle, even as we sleep. I'm kind of getting used to it, so when they bang, we just speak louder. *(music builds;* ANGELA *dances, then sits on floor)* The hiss from the valve makes you feel like someone else is in the room. I say that's the dragon sleeping next to me. You know, it is curious to know that strangers live under our floor and above our heads, and that our own heater pipe goes through everyone's apartments. *(music stops)* I miss our house in Puerto Rico. Your Angela."

(band plays a bolero; FATHER *walks downstage from behind scrim;* MOTHER *fixes* BILLY's *vest; behind scrim* ANGELA *caresses her father's Navy uniform while he speaks downstage in front of the scrim)*

FATHER   "Dear Brother, I have learned some painful lessons about prejudice while searching for the apartment. But I don't want to tell anybody. Maybe someday. So many of us coming over. Things are changing in these neighborhoods, and people are panicking over here. I went to look for an apartment, put on my Navy uniform to look my best." *(*NELSON *and* BILLY *enter from behind their scrims and walk downstage, joining* FATHER*)* "This man looks at my name tag, points his finger at it, and asks, 'You Cuban?' 'No,' I answered, looking past the finger and into his angry eyes. 'I'm Puerto Rican.' *(pause;* BILLY *and* NELSON *react, each in their own world)* And the door closed. *(*BILLY *and* NELSON *retreat;* FATHER *looks at* ANGELA*)* I wonder what will happen in this neighborhood if more Puerto Ricans continue to come here. For now, we are keeping busy with a New Year's Eve party, since we can't go to Puerto Rico. We'll have a good crowd of friends—Uncle Germán, our cousins, and the kids. Our nephew will introduce his eighteen-year-old girlfriend to the family. I'll let you know how that goes. She just arrived from Puerto Rico." *(lights fade)*

Scene 9

(band plays "Greenwood Side'eo"; lights with Appalachian patterns projected over all three scrims; curtains are closed; MOTHER *and* BILLY *venture out of their world and into the other playing areas—looking, discovering, and wondering;* BILLY *wears his new vest, and* MOTHER *is dressed up in a hat and blazer; for a moment, they stop upstage center in front of the band)*

MOTHER *(walking downstage center)* Tell you the truth, this world is a big ball to me. I don't know how people ever got anywhere. I'd never been nowhere, much less to a place like that University Hospital, but from the time Billy was eleven 'til he was eighteen we went ever' three months. He had whooping cough, and it affected his brain. They said they found a black streak in his brain from coughin' so hard, but they said they couldn't operate or he'd be in worser shape. If that was now, they'd do something, but it's too late. *(*BILLY *angrily rushes off to his Appalachian home)* If he lives 'til fall, he'll be sixty-five. *(she observes* BILLY; *lights up on him as he sings)*

BILLY
To market, to market to buy a fat hog
Jiggety, jiggety, jiggety jog.

One of them said, "What's wrong with this'n?" Other'n said, "I don't know, some kind of fits. You know them hillbillies, probably married her uncle." I asked that'n if he was my pa or my uncle. She said, "Don't ask foolish questions!" At first it was fun to go, but I was glad when we quit.

MOTHER   They said there was nothin' more they could do. We could get his medicine from any doctor, and I could give it to him. *(MOTHER takes off her hat and crosses behind Appalachian scrim, forming a silhouette; lights rise on* MOTHER *singing "Greenwood Side'eo")*

Then she drew out her wee penknife
All alee and lonely.
There she took those wee babes' lives
Down by the Greenwood side'eo.

BILLY   I tried to go back to school, but that'n said no. She just wanted me to stay home and work.

MOTHER   *(enters and gives* BILLY *a pot and spoon to batter)* He'd slip off and they'd send one of the other children after me to come get him.

BILLY   *(waits for her to leave; puts down pot and spoon)* At recess they played a game, the boys and girls together—housekeeping. I wanted to play housekeeping with my danged ol' sweetheart Serecea, but she didn't want to.

MOTHER   *(lights up on* MOTHER; *she gives him pot and spoon; indicates that he should continue to batter)* He like to wore me out. Ever' day was a rasslin' match. Tryin' to raise seven others, cook, farm, can. One day, I'd been up 'fore daylight, canning beans outside in a tub. Well, this woman from the health department come by to see about Billy, and I just didn't have time to talk to her. She said, "My God. You work like a brute!"

Lord, that flew all over me. I ain't no brute. A brute is a dumb animal that has to be drove to work. Nobody drove me. I worked hard for a reason, my own reasons. Me and Billy, we ain't no mindless brutes. But one day, later on up in early winter, I was feeding the livestock, and I was plumb wore out. I was cold, and so tired I like to have cried. All the sheep was laying down in a stall. They looked so warm and restful all laying there together, and I real careful laid down, curled up next to 'em, and they let me. I slept for about an hour. When I woke up, I thought, Lord, that woman was right. I've become a brute. When I went back up to the house, my husband said, "Where in the world have you been? You stink like sheep."

(MOTHER *teases* BILLY; *light on her fades;* BILLY *sings*)

BILLY

Baa, baa black sheep
Have you any wool?
Yes sir, yes sir
Don't be cruel
To a heart that's true.

(ANGELA *is in New York tenement in silhouette, brushing her hair; band plays "Bus Ride"*)

BILLY   Serecea started goin' to that town school, and they wouldn't let me ride the bus. All them other'ns rode the bus, why couldn't I? I told that'n I wanted to marry Serecea. That'n said, "I reckon not." So I decided to ask Serecea. I went down to where them Vanover children lived. They was a whole mess of them, and I got on the bus with 'em and I found Serecea and I set next to her all the way to town, but I couldn't git up the nerve to ask her. So we set, not sayin' nothin' and ever'body starin' at us. And when we got to town she got off, and I stayed to save her seat so's I could ask her goin' home. But some of them come an' said, "Git off!" "This'n'll just set right here, thank ye." "Fine, just set there all day, then." And I did. It was hard, but I did. Then come time to go home and the policeman come and said, "Git off!" And I locked hold on the seat rail in front of me, and I held on and they beat my knuckles 'til they bled and I held on and one of them said, "They'll raise a fuss about us beatin' up a dummy. Let's just take the seats out." And they did and they carried me out. All of the others was lined up outside and there was Serecea in front and I said,

"Well, hello, danged ol' sweetheart." *(music turns discordant;* MOTHER *and* DONNA *appear behind their scrims)* And she slapped me . . . *("Bus Ride" ends; all three women stand in silhouette, as if staring out a window)* hard in the face. Everybody laughed. This'n did, too."

(New York light patterns appear over all scrims; silence; all curtains open)

Scene 10

ANGELA   *(teenage* ANGELA *peeks out from behind scrim)* "Dear Gramma, you wouldn't recognize this neighborhood. *(congas play;* ANGELA *enters from behind scrim; walks downstage)* Remember when we first moved here and you came to visit? Well, now it is mainly a Puerto Rican neighborhood. It is as if the heart of the city map was being gradually colored in brown. Papi's obsession with getting us out of here is getting to me. He doesn't want us to have friends because 'we'll be moving out soon.' But it's heaven for Mami." *(band plays "Dear Gramma";* ANGELA *dances all over the stage in awe of her city's tall buildings and crowds of people)*

ANGELA   *(sings)*
Gramma, let me tell you
What is like to live in New York.

ANGELA   "Papi always wants us to do our grocery shopping at the super-market when he comes home on weekend leaves, but Mami insists that she can cook only with products whose labels she can read, so during the week I go with her to la bodega across the street from el building. Ah, and have I told you that the final *e* is not pronounced for Palmolive and Colgate the way we do it in Spanish? For years I believed that they were Puerto Rican products. Imagine my surprise at first hearing a com-mercial on television for Colg*ate* and Palmolive. I have to run. Bye, your favorite, Angela."

(ANGELA sings; the rest of cast all sing the chorus and dance behind scrims)

ANGELA

Gramma, let me tell you
What it's like to live in New York.

ALL

Gramma, let me tell you
What it's like to live in New York.

(cast continues to sing refrain; FATHER comes from behind scrim, wearing his Navy uniform, and stands downstage center)

Gramma, let me tell you
What it's like to live in New York.

(music ends)

FATHER *(ANGELA, as an adult, observes FATHER, as if looking back into a memory)* I devised a system of back-and-forth travel. Every time I am sent to Europe, you will go back to Puerto Rico with your grandmother. Upon my return to Brooklyn Yard, I will wire you, and you will come back.

(band plays "Strangers," an Appalachian ballad)

ANGELA *(as she speaks, ANGELA stares at a uniformed image of her FATHER; FATHER turns around with military precision)* My father was a man who rarely looked into mirrors. What was he afraid of seeing? My mother prefers to remember him as the golden boy she married. He was a sensitive man, whose energies had to be entirely devoted to survival. And that is how many minds are wasted in the travails of immigrant life. *(lights fade; curtain is drawn)*

Scene 11

(band plays "Sincerely Yours" with an African flair; lights come up on NELSON *and* DONNA *behind New Orleans shotgun house scrim; they face each other in silhouette)*

NELSON   *(sings)*

> If I could promise you a love song
> I'd cup my hands to catch the sound of clear running water
> Bubbling through a bed of stone and pebble
> And bring it to the sunny place that you make laughing.
> I'd make a song that lights up the air the way your laughter
>   does
> If I could promise you a love song.

(it's African Liberation Day, 1971; music transitions to "African Liberation Day Theme"; DONNA *opens curtain on New York tenement scrim;* NELSON *is concluding a speech in Shakespeare Park; crowd behind scrims cheers him on, fists up; shadows of crowd reflected on the walls)*

NELSON   We've got a right to be proud of what we've done on this African Liberation Day. We're over two thousand strong here today. Next year we need to double our numbers if we want "South Africa for '73." 1971 is not the end. 1971 is a new beginning. But the best way we can help our brothers and sisters in Africa is to win the fight for justice here at home. So what if it's true that white folk are guilty of making slaves of us back in the day, and ripping off the riches of Africa with colonialism; we need to understand all that, but let's not get bogged down in bitterness and anger, because the future is in our hands. We're the only ones who can make ourselves free. "South Africa Free by '73." *(lights out behind scrims; lights up on* NELSON *now in New Orleans shotgun house;* DONNA *enters carrying two coats and hats)* Look at that crowd, DiDi! This is the best African Liberation Day ever.

DONNA Come on in the church office. Here, you need to put this on. *(gives* NELSON *trench coat, hat, and sunglasses)*

NELSON *(makes believe he is putting them on, joking)* What's this stuff? This ain't no Mardi Gras!

DONNA *(putting on her coat)* Just put it on, please. The federal court rejected our appeal. They refused to set aside your conviction. If you stay here, these crackers will throw the book at you. So as your legal counsel, I say you better get the hell out of here.

NELSON We got people out there from every major Black organization inside of two hundred miles. If I leave now, the whole thing could fall apart.

DONNA Any movement that depends on one man is no better than a one-man army.

NELSON Where do you think I ought to go?

DONNA We've got options. First stop is in Mexico. Then Cuba, Algeria, China. Here are passports, money; everything we'll need is in the car.

NELSON They'd know you were involved. You'd lose you license to practice law.

DONNA Attorney-client privilege, not to mention that they'd have to prove that I did something illegal. But that's all moot anyway. I'm going with you.

NELSON Is this still my lawyer talking?

DONNA No. It's the mother of your unborn child.

NELSON The mother of my . . . DiDi. *You gros com sa?* You don't mean I'm pregnant?

DONNA No, fool. *I'm* pregnant.

NELSON I'm gonna— Hey, Rev! Somebody! I'm—we're going to have a baby. Come here, woman. We definitely got something to celebrate now.

DONNA We'll have plenty of time to celebrate when we get to Mexico. Hurry up. Get changed.

NELSON DiDi, I can't do that. *(takes off sunglasses and hat)*

DONNA   You don't understand the urgency of the problem here.

NELSON   Don't ever tell me what I don't understand! Do you hear me? What would I do in Cuba or Algeria or China? Or Africa, as far as that's concerned?

DONNA   What will you do in jail for the next thirty years?

NELSON   The same thing that Mandela's doing on Robben Island, standing on principle.

DONNA   And what about me?

NELSON   You would not want a man who compromises on principle.

DONNA   What about our child?

NELSON   We'll love the child, DiDi. That's what we'll do. And we'll teach the kid to love our people, and to love the struggle for justice.

DONNA   You'll be in jail, at best. What kind of father can you be sitting in jail?

NELSON   *(embracing her)* I've got the best lawyer in the world. If they get me in jail, she won't let me stay in jail any longer that I have to, will you, baby? Come on, baby, let's go tell the people we going to have a new soldier for the revolution! *("African Liberation Day Theme" ends; lights fade)*

Scene 12

MOTHER   *(lights come up on the rural Appalachian house;* MOTHER *enters and dusts furniture with a rag;* DONNA *sits in front of New Orleans shotgun house scrim, rocking baby in dim light)* About the time Billy thought he was growed up, he wanted to go out on his own. Whenever he'd see his brothers and sisters goin' off, it was hard on him. He never saw the difference between him and them. I tried my best to explain it, but I don't understand, either. There are some things in this life we are not meant to understand. You don't have to understand everything for it to be so and have a place in this world. Maybe that's what God is—understanding. *(*MOTHER *comes from behind scrim; walks downstage)* One of my daughter-in-laws was here one time, and I had about a six-foot blacksnake skin layin' out on the walk. I told her I found it under the house, where I keep my taters. "Lord have mercy, you mean there's a six-foot blacksnake living under your house? I would not stay here one minute. How can you live knowing that?" Ever'thing don't exist for my use and purpose. Some things have meaning beyond my knowing about it. That snake's one of 'em. But I admit, if I run up on him, he's liable to end up dead, 'cause I reckon they's things about me that snake don't understand, either.

(MOTHER *returns behind scrim; light fades on her and* DONNA; *lights up on* BILLY *singing)*

BILLY
    Dim lights, thick smoke
    And loud, loud music.
    You'll never make a wife
    To a home-lovin' man.

There was one of them women in town and she had big breasts that she showed half of 'em and I was there one day gettin' a hot dog and a Grapette and she bent over and I pinched her on the breast and she screamed real loud and a man run up and this'n hit him in the pit of the stomach with my balled-up fist and he got this funny look on his face and fell over. And this'n started laughing and the woman was screaming and this'n pinched the other'n and she slapped me and I grabbed her and squeezed her real tight 'til her breasts popped out *(lights up on* MOTHER *staring at him)* and everybody was hollerin' and this'n felt so good.

(band plays instrumental bolero; BILLY *picks up his banjo and hugs it as though he is dancing with it; he swings around and sees* MOTHER, *who is watching him; he realizes she has heard him and moves to background shyly)*

MOTHER They told me if he come back, they'd have no course but to put him in jail. The doctor said his body was changin' and all they could do was change his medicine and maybe it would help, but ever'body but me was afraid of him.

(MOTHER *sings*)

> She rubbed the knife against her shoe
> All alee and lonely
> The more she rubbed the redder it grew
> Down by the Greenwood side'eo.

(MOTHER *sits*)

The longest I've ever been away from him was three weeks when my oldest girl got real sick and I had to go stay with her. He whipped all his brothers. The girls left and stayed with family. Rocked my husband for half a day and kept him penned up in the barn. When I come home, Wes said, "Next time we're just gonna burn the place down and come with you."

(*lights up on* BILLY *clutching his banjo, singing softly*)

BILLY
> Yes, I've been around the world
> But I never found no girl.
> I'm a wise boy, but some boys are silly.

MOTHER   Some boys are just silly.

(*lights fade; lights rise on* DONNA *seated in front of the New Orleans shotgun house scrim, holding the baby; a jail pattern is projected over the scrim;* NELSON *is behind the scrim, in jail, reading a book*)

DONNA   Some boys are just silly.

(DONNA *sings*)

> Hush, little baby, don't you cry
> You know your daddy
> Is bound to die.
> All our trials will soon be over.

(lights fade; lights rise on FATHER *behind New York tenement scrim;* ANGELA *walks from behind scrim to downstage; she watches* FATHER *as if he's a memory)*

FATHER   Estoy tratando de que nos asimilemos lo mejor posible. Acabo de comprar y cargar un árbol de Navidad cinco pisos hasta nuestro apartamento y ustedes son los únicos en el building que reciben regalo de Navidad y de Día de Reyes. Además, tenemos el mayor de los lujos . . . nuestro propio televisor. Hey, ya estamos en los '60. *(musician plays chords of "Middle America" behind rural Appalachian house scrim)* We are one of the first families in the barrio to have one. And it keeps you kids inside the house. Compared to our neighbors in el building, we are rich. The Navy check is better than a factory check. The only thing is, I still can't buy a place away from the barrio. My greatest wish.

(a musician enters playing guitar)

ANGELA   His greatest wish was Mami's greatest fear—to live away from the barrio! The TV did help to keep us quiet inside the apartment. I love the family series. My favorite is *Bachelor Father,* where the father treats his adopted teenage daughter like a princess because he is rich and has a Chinese houseboy to do everything for him. Then there is *Father Knows Best* and *Leave It to Beaver.* It was like a map of Middle America. *(walks to trunk and stands on it; lights fade)*

Scene 13

(spotlight on a musician; he sings)

MUSICIAN
   The lives we live
   Are paid for by our children.
   The dreams we dream
   Slowly fade away.

Still, we dance each dance
Like it was the first time.
But the fiddler's waiting
And he has to be paid.
Deep in the heart
Of Middle America
There's a two-for-one sale
A midnight madness jubilee.
You can get it all here
Love, hope, and happiness.
It's all for sale
Satisfaction not guaranteed.

(lights come up on New Orleans house; MUSICIAN *walks over to* DONNA *sitting, holding the baby as she sings)*

DONNA

There are some things
We can never understand
How a man loves a woman
And a woman loves a man.
Are angels real?
Does God really have a plan?
How can some people live
And never seem to give a damn.

DONNA & MUSICIAN

Deep in the heart
Of Middle America
There's a two-for-one sale
A midnight madness jubilee.
You can get it all here
Love, hope, and happiness.
It's all for sale
Satisfaction not guaranteed.

(lights up on New York tenement; FATHER *is singing; musician walks over and joins him)*

FATHER & MUSICIAN

This is not my home
I'm a stranger here.
Wherever I travel
I carry my home there.
This is not my voice
No one listens anymore.
Deep in my heart I hear
A song from the other shore.

ENTIRE CAST

Deep in the heart
Of Middle America
There's a two-for-one sale
A midnight madness jubilee.
You can get it all here
Love, hope and happiness.
It's all for sale
Satisfaction not guaranteed.

(blackout)

—— **INTERMISSION** ——

ACT 2

Scene 1

(playing area curtains are closed; banjo is placed on trunk in front of the rural Appalachian house scrim; there are folded letters placed on the trunk

in front of the New York tenement house scrim; spotlight rises on an Appa-
lachian musician playing an Irish drum; he freezes; spotlight fades; spotlight
rises on a Puerto Rican musician as he plays the congas in front of the
New York tenement scrim; he freezes; spotlight fades; spotlight rises on an
African American musician as he plays a tambourine in front of the New
Orleans shotgun house scrim; he freezes; spotlight fades; a spotlight rises on
a drummer in the band as he plays a trap set; a keyboardist and bass player
join in and play the entr'acte; as the musical number reaches its peak, cast
members enter and take their places behind their respective scrims; band
plays "Mardi Grasly Yours"; DONNA *sings over the music)*

DONNA   *(in silhouette behind scrim)*
   If I could promise you a love song
   I'd take the time to count the ways that love makes music
   I'd take the days and stretch them out before your very feet
   I'd take the nights' soft velvet sheets
   To wrap your dreams in
   If I could promise you a love song.

(music cross fades from "Mardi Grasly Yours" to "Meters Groove"; DONNA
and NELSON *enter between two scrims, dancing; other actors dance in sil-*
houette behind their scrims; DONNA *and* NELSON *are guests of honor at the*
Nubian Knights Ball; it has just been announced that they will be King and
Queen of Nubian Knights for the next Carnival; their son, DONALD, *and his*
band are playing for the ball; "Meters Groove" ends; lights rise to a bright
glow on the New Orleans shotgun house; DONNA *and* NELSON *acknowledge*
the presence and greetings of the others throughout the scene)

NELSON   *(wearing a fake smile)* I don't know why in the hell I let you
convince me to be the King of a reactionary Mardi Gras club like this.

DONNA   *(also smiling)* It would have been rude to refuse the honor of
having been elected King and Queen.

NELSON   *(to a person at the ball)* Hey, thanks, brother man! Thanks for
your support.

DONNA   If the All African People's Coalition really wants to impact electoral politics, these are some of the key people you'll have to deal with. Maybe they won't be with you, but you definitely don't want them working against you.

DONALD   *(entering from band area)* Hey, Mom. Hey, Pops. They're really putting on the dog for y'all tonight.

NELSON   Hold up. The brother wants a picture of the royal family. *(pose for picture)*

DONNA   You're sounding really good tonight, son.

NELSON   Thank you, brother.

DONALD   Aw, you're just prejudiced, Mom. Everybody knows you're my number-one fan.

DONNA   And proud of it, too!

NELSON   Your music is fine. Everybody loves it. So why you got to go to a music school? You ought to study something substantial, like math or science or history. Something that will help you be a better leader for our struggle.

DONNA   Nelson! This is neither the time nor the place.

NELSON   It's always the time for struggle. It's always the place. No one is . . .

DONNA & DONALD   free until all are free!

DONNA   For heaven's sake, Nelson, this is a party and we're the guests of honor.

NELSON   Which makes it all the more important for us to stay focused. His generation's got a lifetime of struggle in front of them. Music is nice, but no revolution was ever won on the bandstand.

DONNA   Our music is the essence of our struggle. When our language, our social structures, our artifacts, and our gods were destroyed, all we were able to hang on to was our music.

DONALD   Mom's right, Daddy. Black music is one of the greatest contributions anybody ever made to world culture. I'll tell you what: Without music, there wouldn't be much of a movement, either.

DONNA Precisely! So if you think the Jazz Academy College will help you develop your talent, son, go right ahead.

NELSON It's not just a question of how to develop our talents. How will our talents work for us? We'd be irresponsible as parents in the struggle . . .

DONNA Irresponsible parents? Now you stop right there, Mr. Nelson "Mandela" Hardiman. Don't you dare raise that issue with me. Where were you when I was pregnant? In jail. Where were you during the first ten years of his life? In jail! (DONALD *returns to bandstand*) Then, when I finally got you out of jail, did you stay home to help? No. You were running all over the place, fighting for the so-called revolution while I was raising our child and making a living for our family. The only time you worried about being a parent was when there was a photo op for the happy family.

NELSON That was a low blow, Donna.

DONNA Donald! Where did he go?

NELSON He had to get back to work. (DONNA *retreats behind scrim of New Orleans home;* NELSON *focuses on guests*) A constant struggle . . . yeah . . . a strong Black woman . . . a constant struggle, brother. Good to see you, man. (*to* DONNA) DiDi! Donna! (*exits behind New Orleans scrim;* NELSON *and* DONNA *stand behind scrim, arguing in silhouette; from bandstand, Donald sings "How Can You Say You Love Me")*

DONALD

How can you say you love me, when you never treat me
  right?
How can you say you love me, when you never treat me
  right?
I always give you what you want, but when it's my turn
  it's a fight.
My mama then told me, "Son, love can be a rocky road."
My mama then told me, "Son, love can be a rocky road."
Just when you give your heart sometimes love will turn
  so cold.
The only question left is whether I'll pack my bags and
  leave.

The only question left is whether I'll pack my bags and
leave.

If you won't treat me right, said I'm moving down the line.

(lights fade on band and New Orleans shotgun house)

Scene 2

(lights rise on New York tenement; FATHER *looks through letters; begins
to read one)*

FATHER "My dearest brother, you are going to miss a great New Year's
Eve party. On Saturday the whole family will walk downtown to shop
at the big department stores on Broadway. I admit that it's easier to go
shopping in el barrio, where your face does not turn a clerk to stone;
where our money is as green as anyone else's. I'll buy a dark suit for
the occasion. It's going to be a big celebration, and everyone is excited
because my wife's brother has bought a movie camera, which he will be
trying out that night. I wish you were here with us. Better yet, I wish we
were in Puerto Rico with you. Your dearest brother."

(band plays "Toda una vida" as FATHER *and* ANGELA *dress up for the party;*
FATHER *wears a suit, vest, and hat;* ANGELA *puts her hair into a ponytail
tied with a red ribbon, and wears a scarf around her hips and a white faux-
fur stole; music ends; they sit on the trunk)*

ANGELA We have a home movie of this party. Several times my mother
and I have watched it together. It is grainy and short. And it is in color.
The only complete scene in color I can recall from those years. The movie
opens with a sweep of the living room. *(movie music; spotlights flicker to
create "movie effect" as* ANGELA *continues;* MOTHER *becomes visible behind
the rural Appalachian scrim, rocking in silhouette;* ANGELA *comes from
behind the scrim and walks downstage;* FATHER *stands on the trunk and
pulls out a roll of red ribbons; he throws the ribbon toward* ANGELA; *she*

catches ribbons and lets them drop to the floor; he throws a second one, and so on) It is typical immigrant Puerto Rican decor for the time. The sofa and chairs are upholstered in bright colors, covered in transparent plastic. The linoleum on the floor is light blue. There are dime-size indentations all over it—victim of the spike heels. *(*ANGELA *continues describing the silent movie, living it as she tells it;* FATHER *stands in front of the trunk, with gestures of handshakes and smiles)* The room is full of people dressed in mainly two colors—dark suits for the men, red dresses for the women. We were dressed up like child models in the Sears catalog. My brother in a miniature man's suit and bow tie, and I in black patent-leather shoes and a frilly dress with several layers of crinolines underneath. The women in red sitting on the couch are my mother and my eighteen-year-old cousin. My cousin has grown up in Paterson and is in her last year of high school. She doesn't have a trace of "la mancha," the mark of the new immigrant. She is wearing a tight red-sequined cocktail dress. *(*ANGELA *and* FATHER *sit on trunk)* Her brown hair has been lightened with peroxide around the bangs, and she is holding a cigarette very expertly between her fingers. *(silhouette of* MOTHER *fades)*

FATHER   *(walking downstage)* She can pass for an American anywhere. At least for Italian anyway. Her life is going to be different. She has an American boyfriend. He is older and has a car. If she marries him, even her name will be American. *(returns to trunk and sits next to* ANGELA*)*

ANGELA   For years I've had dreams and nightmares in the form of this home movie. Familiar faces pushing themselves forward into my mind. Like this old woman, whose mouth becomes a cavernous black hole I fall into, and as I fall, I can feel her laughter.

(band plays "Old Woman" as ANGELA *becomes the old woman of her nightmares; they walk downstage close together in the same rhythm, speaking simultaneously)*

FATHER & ANGELA
  Your cousin is pregnant by that man
  She's been sneaking around with.

Would I lie to you?
I was not invited to this party,
But I came anyway.
Your cousin is growing a gringuito in her belly.
She put something long and
Pointy into her pretty self.
Hmmm.
And they probably flushed it down
the toilet.
The father does not want that baby.
He is growing real children,
With a wife who is
A natural blonde.
And guess where your cousin will end?
Hmmm?
She'll be sent to a small town
In Puerto Rico.
A real change in scenery.
La Gringa, they'll call her over there.
Ha, ha, ha.
La Gringa is what she always wanted to be!

Scene 3

(soft light comes up on the band; DONALD, *now a successful musician, steps downstage playing "Serenade"; he crosses to the Appalachian house, where a soft glow illuminates* MOTHER *and* BILLY *exchanging gifts;* MOTHER *gives* BILLY *an orange; he gives her a red ribbon for her hair; lights fade as* DONALD *crosses to the New York tenement; lights come up on* FATHER *and* ANGELA; *she sits on trunk, where* FATHER *places a small package of old letters tied with red ribbon, and leaves;* DONALD *continues to play for* ANGELA; *lights fade, then come up on the New Orleans shotgun house, where* DONALD *now plays;* NELSON *and* DONNA *sit together; "Serenade" ends; spotlight on* DONALD *fades; it's Christmas 1998)*

DONNA   Donald! This makes my holiday complete! You're supposed to be on tour with the band.

DONALD   I am, but I arranged a layover so I could see you guys for a couple of hours. Where've you been? I thought I was going to miss you.

DONNA   We were with cousin Maudine and her family, celebrating Kwanzaa. She's got the sweetest little grandchild.

NELSON   Hey, it's great that you're here. I'm doing a fund-raiser on "Creativity Night." You can be our guest star.

DONALD   I'm really sorry, Pops. I've got to split tonight. I'm headlining a benefit on New Year's Eve for the South African Children's Fund.

NELSON   Oh, I see.

DONNA   That's wonderful, dear.

DONALD   Yeah, yeah. Yo, dig. There're a couple of things I want to drop on y'all. This is for you, Pops. *(hands him an envelope)*

NELSON   What's this?

DONALD   Go on. Open it.

NELSON   What in the world?

DONALD   You know my latest album, *Star-Crossed Lovers,* it went platinum last week. That's practically unheard of in jazz, so I'm doing alright. So, Pops, considering how hard you've worked all your life to keep the All African People's deal afloat, I told my agent to sign the royalties from this album over to you. That's your first payment.

NELSON   I don't know what to say.

DONNA   "Thanks" is what people normally say in a situation like this.

NELSON   Thanks, son. *(they embrace)*

DONALD   I thought it would let a little pressure off you, Mom. (DONALD *kisses* DONNA) The other thing I wanted you guys to know is that I'm planning to get married. *(band plays soft conga and bass rhythm)*

DONNA   Oh, baby, that's wonderful!

NELSON   Who is the lucky girl?

DONNA   Do we know her?

DONALD   Nah, I don't think so. Here's her picture. I met her in New York. She hasn't come down here yet. She's dying to find out about New Orleans, though.

DONNA   *(looking at photo)* Donald, you're not serious about this, are you?

NELSON   What's wrong?

DONNA   What's wrong?

DONALD   There it is!

DONNA   This is a white girl! That's what's wrong!

DONALD   She's not white.

DONNA   Natural blonde and with baby blue eyes. If she's not white, you have a real serious problem, 'cause Creole wannabes are worse than real white folk.

NELSON   Let's try to get a handle on the big picture here.

DONNA   Nelson, you take your handle and stick it where the sun don't shine. I didn't struggle through life to raise what I thought was a strong, intelligent Black man to have him run off with some no-count white girl.

NELSON   Donna . . .

DONALD   She's not white, Mom. She's Puerto Rican. *(music stops)*

DONNA   That makes a whole lot of difference, huh!

NELSON   The African cultural influence is very strong in Puerto Rican culture. They have a whole different take on race. I have some very strong comrades in the Movement.

DONNA   This is not about some abstract movement. This is about my son. And I don't want half-white grandchildren who think they can be white if they want to.

NELSON   It's not a question of skin color, Donna, it's a question of consciousness. Does she understand the relationship between class, race, and the struggle for justice? What does she think about . . .

DONALD   She thinks I love her! And I think she loves me. And that wraps it. This is my life. I'm not just the focus of your arguments about politics. I'm flesh and blood and feelings. And I'm a horn player, a jazzman. That's all. *(DONNA turns her back to NELSON and DONALD)* Look. I love you guys, but I got to go. I'll let you know when the wedding is. I guess we'll have to do it in New York. If you think you can handle it, you'll be welcome. I won't bring her down here 'til I feel like you'll be comfortable with her. *(DONALD is leaving as* NELSON *makes a pleading gesture for him to come closer to his mother;* DONALD *gives her a quick kiss; she does not respond; he exits)*

DONNA   Where did I go wrong? Lord knows I did the best I could do. I needed more help from you.

NELSON   You sound like it's all over. We're not done yet. *(he tries to embrace her)*

DONNA   Aren't we? *(lights fade)*

Scene 4

(lights on the rural Appalachian house; MOTHER *and* BILLY *are arguing)*

BILLY   *(chasing* MOTHER *around; agitated)* You think them's not this'n, don't you? This'n couldn't be that or know 'bout this or understand that—why not? Why can't I be anybody? I got no credit, no driver's license, no car, no job, no children, no wife, no debts, no house, no money, no sense, no future, no past. If this'n is whatever you think I am, then why can't I be whatever I think I am? Why can't this'n? *(BILLY exits, leaving* MOTHER *onstage)*

(lights rise on New York tenement house; FATHER *is singing a capella "La última copa")*

FATHER
    Eche amigo, no más écheme, llene,
    hasta el borde la copa de champagne
    que esta noche de farra y alegría
    el dolor de mi alma quiero ahogar.
    Es la última farra de mi vida,
    de mi vida, muchachos, que se va,
    mejor dicho que se ha ido tras de aquella,
    que no supo mi amor nunca apreciar.

(he continues singing as spotlight rises on MOTHER *singing "Greenwood Side'eo" a capella; overlapping with* FATHER*)*

MOTHER

> Then she returned to her father's hall
> All alee and lonely.
> Saw two babes a-playing at ball
> Down by the Greenwood side'eo.
> O' babes, o' babes, if you were mine
> All alee and lonely.
> I'd dress you up in scarlet fine
> Down by the Greenwood side'eo.

Besides the Lord, it is this land that has been the most comfort to me. And it is Billy who has helped me to stay here. The only time my husband ever spoke directly to me in forty-four years to tell me to do somethin' was to buy this land when we get the chance. Land is about raising family, generation after generation, not just its coal and timber—ground for one generation to use up. You don't say I'll be a mother 'til this child goes off on its own, then I won't be its mother. It ain't no short-term thing. I'll live here on this land 'til I don't need it no more, then I'll just stop caring for it?

FATHER   "Dear Brother: It was a great party after all. Lots of food, pasteles, gandules, and the rice with the real sofrito you sent up from the island. We can never find sofrito here. Maybe someday we'll sell the stuff ourselves. Oh, there was lots of rum, lots of Palo Viejo, lots of dominó. The more we played and drank, the more we cried. I didn't cry, nor drink. But you know, at midnight some people were reminded of the island by the smells in the kitchen . . . you know . . . oh, and the music. We played Daniel Santos, Felipe Rodríguez . . . *(sings)*

> Eche amigo, no mas écheme, llena,
> hasta el borde la copa de champagne
> que esta noche de farra y alegría
> el dolor de mi alma quiero ahogar.

(FATHER *hums as band starts to play "Sincerely Yours"; lights on New York tenement fade;* NELSON *and* DONNA *appear behind New Orleans shotgun house scrim in silhouette)*

NELSON & DONNA *(sing)*
 But such songs of love belong to men
 Who seek the simple end of pleasure.
 Though pleasure's sweet
 Lovers still are meat and bone
 Don't live alone
 And, like water drops, have histories.

Scene 5

(three pools of light illuminate scrims; as if in a silent movie, BILLY *sits playing banjo for* MOTHER, *though it cannot be heard;* MOTHER *dances;* FATHER *dances downstage of New York tenement scrim;* DONNA *and* NELSON *dance downstage of the New Orleans shotgun house scrim; all dance in slow motion;* ANGELA *dances slowly downstage, then stands)*

ANGELA The five-minute home movie ends with people dancing in a circle. My uncle, the creative filmmaker, must have asked them to do that so they could file past him. You can't justify the absurd movements. People appear frantic, their faces embarrassingly intense. For years I've had dreams and nightmares in the form of this home movie. There is no music in my dream. I hear the dead and the forgotten speak. Familiar faces pushing themselves forward into my mind. A conga line that keeps moving silently past me. It is comical and sad to watch silent dancing. *(pause)* Move back, Uncle. Give the dancers room to move. Soon it will be midnight. *(lights on* ANGELA *quickly fade; lights fade on others dancing slowly)*

Scene 6

(lights come up on rural Appalachian house, where BILLY *is playing banjo loudly, and* MOTHER *is dancing excitedly)*

MOTHER   *(out of breath)* I got eight children, twenty-seven grandchildren, fifteen great-grandchildren, and nineteen and a half acres to divide among 'em. Now they ain't gonna get much if that's how they look at it. But as a whole, it's still as important as when we come here, maybe more so. There's something to be said for looking at life as a whole thing, at looking at this world as a whole thing. You take the hard things and the good things and you make a life out of 'em. Billy taught me that.

I count every day a blessing that I can get up and fix him something to eat. He's been a great comfort to me. He's never been a burden. I know somebody else won't understand me saying that, but he's here no matter whatever else happens. He's here for me. I'm eighty-eight years old, though it don't seem that long somehow. 'Bout ever'body I growed up with is gone. My husband, Mommy, Daddy, brothers, sisters, friends, all gone. The hardest part is having nobody to share your memories with. Somebody who knows what you know without you having to explain it to 'em. My children are all living, but they're sprangled out like a bean vine all over this here country. Except Billy. Somebody said one time, "I don't see why you don't put him in a home, so one time in your life you'd be free." Without Billy, I'd be just another old woman. Without Billy, they'd a-moved me from here long ago. Free? Well, I don't want to be free! Free of love?

BILLY   *(sings)*
There was a lady lived in York
Billy Boy, Billy Boy.

*(*MOTHER *comes to* BILLY; *he embraces her softly)*

BILLY   This'n here don't remember. That'n says she does and I guess she does. When it comes to it, if you can believe one, that's good. Them ain't got nothin' to do with it. Us ain't got nothin' to do with it. This'n and that'n, that's all they is.

BILLY & MOTHER   *(sing)*
She loved him up, she loved him down
All alee and lonely.
Loved him 'til he filled her heart
Down by the Greenwood side'eo.

(MOTHER *rests her head on* BILLY's *shoulder; lights fade on the rural Appalachian house; silhouettes and patterns come up on all three scrims;* BILLY *and* MOTHER *face each other, joining hands;* FATHER *and* ANGELA *face each other, with her standing at a distance;* DONNA *and* NELSON *stand side by side*)

DONNA & NELSON   *(sing)*
> The price of peace is charged in blood
> And this a time for struggle,
> When love songs made of fluffy stuff
> Turn dry and brittle
> Blow away.
> What good's a parasol in heavy rain?
> A dainty cake to starving masses?
> Did crazed Nero stain his place in time
> With Love's lyric?
> All light unweighted things,
> Like feathers, flutter in the wind.

Scene 7

(FATHER *is dressed in white behind the New York tenement scrim;* ANGELA *sits on the trunk, her back to the audience, looking at* FATHER)

FATHER   It is a dangerous thing to forget the climate of your birthplace—to choke out the voices of dead relatives when in dreams they call you by your secret name. It is dangerous to use weapons and sharp instruments you are not familiar with. *(slowly takes off the white hat and suit)* It is dangerous to disdain the plaster saints before which your mother kneels, praying with embarrassing fervor that you survive in the place you have chosen to live. *(lights fade on* FATHER)

ANGELA   Jesús, María y José. To forget is a dangerous thing.

(NELSON *comes from behind New Orleans scrim and crosses to* ANGELA; ANGELA *gets up and joins him; they address the audience*)

NELSON   Read these living words.

ANGELA   Love the lives these words are made of.

NELSON   Know these lives to be your own.

ANGELA   And then, you'll know a love song.

ANGELA & NELSON   *(sing)*
    Made of sweat and bread and blood.
    You sing the tune you know I would
    If I could promise you a love song.

(lights on a musician who enters playing guitar)

ENTIRE CAST   *(sing)*
    If you were me
    And I was you,
    Would I still do
    The things I do?
    Would you still say
    The words you say?
    Would we feel joy?
    Would we feel pain?
    Would every day
    Still start the same,
    A hope and a prayer
    For a love that's true?
    If you were me
    And I was you.
    There is no cure,
    No magic pill
    That can change
    Every ill.
    But . . . maybe
    If we could see
    What it's like
    To be you and me . . .

If you were me
And I was you
Would I be black,
Would you be blue,
To see what life
Put me through?
What would you do?
Would I hide my face
In shame
Every time I heard my name?
Could we both
Stand up proud and true
If you were me
And I was you?
Would we both laugh?
Would we both cry?
Wipe the tears from our eyes,
Give it just one more try
Or two?
If you were me
And I was you.

(cast walks toward audience as it sings last two verses; band plays finale as cast takes a bow; cast breaks the line to dance with one another; they dance as they exit, leaving the band playing until song ends)

——— **END** ———

As If You Yourselves Were Suffering

Preston Mitchell

Remember those in prison as if you were together with them in prison,
and those who are mistreated as if you yourselves were suffering.
—Hebrews 13:3

It seemed like it would be a typical potluck supper for a group of folks at
the Wesley Center on the campus of the University of Virginia's College
at Wise. "We'll grab some pizzas and dessert—be there about six," Willie
had said over the phone. As an Episcopal deacon serving the parishes in
the far southwestern corner of Virginia, my calling and role was to spread
the good news of the love of Jesus Christ. I asked Willie what I could do
for the group. He said, "Bring a salad."

The darkness of the December Saturday night fell early, and the
building was empty when I arrived a few minutes before six. Closer to
six-thirty, a tired yet strangely energized group of twelve mostly elderly
Black women entered the Methodist student center's big dining hall. Willie followed five minutes later with a stack of pizza boxes and a cake to
set beside my salad there on the kitchen counter.

The twelve arrivals had left the previous evening from Richmond,
Virginia, in a fifteen-passenger van driven by Willie's colleague Sylvia,

a young employee of Appalshop, an Appalachian regional arts and humanities center on the Kentucky side of Pine Mountain. After their overnight drive and a full day of visitation with their incarcerated fathers, sons, grandsons, and husbands, the visitors were ready for a good night's rest at the local motel. Their second visitation would be the next morning, Sunday, and then there would be the long ride home.

After Saturday-night dinner and before our good nights, the group sat in a circle to reflect on the day. Most visitors simply identified themselves and thanked the people responsible for reaching out and making the weekend trip possible. But one of them, Shirley, offered more detail, explaining how her day had begun Friday morning as she made her way to Washington, D.C.'s Union Station to catch a Greyhound to Richmond, where she was promised a van would carry her overnight into the unfamiliar mountains. There was a hesitation as a tear formed in her right eye and a crack in her voice. "Today, I saw my son for the first time in twenty-five years." She stopped and dabbed a tissue in one eye and then the other. "I can't begin to tell you how happy, truly happy, I felt." Looking at Sylvia, she said, "Thank you, thank you for giving me today."

● ● ●

In late 1998 and early 1999, two super-maximum-security prisons, Red Onion and Wallens Ridge, opened in rural Wise County, where I had taught history and coached basketball at two county high schools and Clinch Valley College for thirty-nine years. Jobs in the coal mines and on the strip-mining sites were disappearing, and the new prisons, which were state-private partnerships, were being sold to us as economic development. A year after the prisons opened, WMMT-FM, Appalshop's noncommercial community radio station, began a program on Monday nights that featured hip-hop. The station's forty-five volunteer DJs typically played the local and regional bluegrass and old-time mountain music in their record collections, so hip-hop was something new for many listeners of the station that branded itself as "the voice of the mountains." The two young white hip-hop DJs were surprised when they started hearing from listeners they didn't even know existed. More than 60 percent of the inmates locked up in Red Onion and Wallens Ridge were African Americans from the cities of eastern and northern Virginia, while the other 37,000 people in Wise County were 97 percent white. One inmate wrote in response to the new program, "Thank you—we've been drowning in a sea of bluegrass in here."

Because Red Onion and Wallens Ridge were maximum-security facilities, prisoners were in twenty-three-hour lockdown. With this in mind, in December the hip-hop DJs offered a toll-free number for families and friends listening on the internet to call in to the station with a holiday message for their incarcerated loved ones. The Christmas program proved so popular in its heartrending simplicity that these "shout-outs" became a weekly feature of the program, which was soon dubbed *Holler to the Hood.*

In 2006, Appalshop released *Up the Ridge,* a film about the building and opening of the Wallens Ridge prison atop an abandoned coal strip-mining site in Big Stone Gap, Virginia. The film documents what happens to an overwhelmingly white rural community and the majority–African American inmates from distant cities when a prison is sited in a chronically poor region. Because these prisons were touted as having the latest design and state-of-the-art technology to hold "the worst of the worst," some states with overflow prison populations began sending some of their inmates to Red Onion and Wallens Ridge. All out-of-staters were charged a higher daily rate, and, as in the hotel business, the greater the occupancy rate, the greater the profit for the prisons' private investors. At one point, Wallens Ridge even filled eighty of its cells with members of the Rastafarian religious sect from the Virgin Islands. Now, twenty-two years later, there are as many Black men incarcerated in our two prisons as there are free Black men and women in our county.

Roadside Theater, the professional theater wing of Appalshop, soon started going across Virginia, showing *Up the Ridge* and organizing families to petition their elected officials to overturn the state's mandatory sentencing and no-parole laws. During these tours, local leaders said they needed something more—like a church service—to help rally their communities. That something turned out to be Roadside's play *Thousand Kites.* As Miss K., a leader in Richmond, would say to the assembled after the premiere of *Kites* at her church, "Yes, pray for us. But also get up and walk with us!"

. . .

That December night, as we cleaned up after our meal at the Wesley Center in Wise, folks mingled inside while the van was warming up outside. I thanked Willie and Sylvia and asked what my local churches might do to aid the program. "Funny you ask," Willie said with a sly grin. Apparently, my reputation for salads was not all he had in mind. "My church [the United Church of Christ in Berea, Kentucky] doesn't think we have the funds to do a trip in the spring. Do you think you guys might help in the effort?" I believe there are times when there is a God moment, moments when the Holy Spirit jumps in and expresses her hope, her love. "We'll take the trip in the spring," I quickly and confidently said. With financial help from two Episcopal churches in the far southwestern part of the state, All Saints in Norton and Christ Church in Big Stone Gap, we organized the first Rideshare in the spring of 2016.

After being invited and attending our churches' first sponsored trip that spring, two more local churches joined in the Saturday-night suppers: the Williams Chapel AME Zion Church in Big Stone Gap and the Cave, a nondenominational interracial church in Norton. The pastors of these two churches, Sandra and Jimmy, are African American, prompting one of the riders to remark half jokingly, "I didn't think there were any Black people in Wise County."

The planning by church volunteers for these prison visitations was extensive. Lists of potential riders had to be collated; public service announcements advertising the upcoming trip produced and aired on the radio; vans (usually two twelve-passenger vans) rented and drivers recruited who were willing and able to drive overnight; motel rooms reserved; and church members signed up to prepare breakfast, brown-bag lunches, and supper.

Janet never missed a trip to see her son in Wallens Ridge and always left a donation before returning home on Sunday. Essie, a rider from Roanoke, was another fixture on the trips, visiting her grandson, who was serving a thirty-five-year sentence at Red Onion. She was often joined by another grandson, who had played football and graduated from the University of Virginia's College at Wise. Essie served as the matriarch of the groups, cautioning what to say, what to wear, and, most of all, emphasizing how one misstep by any group member could cause the prisons to go into full lockdown and cancel the visit for everyone else, too.

Rasheed's identical twin brother was in his fiftieth year of a life sentence, making him the longest-serving inmate in the state's prison system. At dinner that first Saturday, Rasheed showed us a Polaroid of himself and his brother taken by one of the guards earlier that day. Less than a week later, our churches received a letter from Rasheed, offering thanks for being "treated with what I consider royalty befitting a dignitary." He continued: "In this day and age of divisiveness and disunity, the spoken words, the prayers, the kinship, fellowship and spirit of brotherhood shown in your place of worship truly exemplifies what America is truly about. This can at times be a seemingly cold and uncaring world but I know God is smiling today."

For the next four years, until the 2020 pandemic hit, our churches sponsored nine trips to Red Onion and Wallens Ridge, and also one to nearby Keen Mountain Correctional Center and Pocahontas Correctional Center in the adjoining rural counties of Buchanan and Tazewell. More than 175 riders took part in these visitation weekends. Without the Rideshare program, many of our middle-aged and elderly riders would not have been able to make the more than six-hour trip across the state. For them, seeing their loved ones for two days was the obvious highlight of the weekend. But for many of the church members, the highlight was the lavish potluck supper spread out on Saturday night, followed by group story sharing and prayer.

• • •

Over the years, friendships were formed, and the people in our churches were able to begin feeling the presence of the inmates locked away in Wallens Ridge and Red Onion. Once invisible, they were now seen for who they were: children of God, and, as such, worthy of God's grace, love, and mercy. Each Sunday during the Episcopal Church's Prayers of the People, we bowed our heads and said, "We pray for all prisoners and captives, especially those at Wallens Ridge and Red Onion; that a spirit of forgiveness may replace vengeance and retribution; and that we, with all the destitute, lonely, and oppressed, may be restored to the fullness of God's grace." The kneeling congregants responded in unison: "God of absolution, hear our prayer."

While our Rideshare program was not an advocacy group for prison reform or inmates' rights, the conversations between the riders themselves and the people in the community often turned to this question: "How can I do more?" In 2020, our two Wise County Episcopal churches joined other local groups in the Wise County and the City of Norton Community Remembrance Project, which was formed in response to the 2019 Virginia Assembly House Joint Resolution No. 655, which acknowledged "with profound regret the existence and acceptance of lynching within the commonwealth." The Virginia resolution joins the national Equal Justice Initiative to call on all communities "to create greater awareness and understanding about racial terror lynching and to begin a necessary conversation that advances truth and reconciliation by working with communities to commemorate and recognize the traumatic era of lynching by collecting soil from lynching sites across the country and erecting historical markers and monuments in these spaces."

The Episcopal Church's Baptismal Covenant challenges us to "strive for justice and peace among all people, and respect the dignity of every human being." Rideshare became a gift, a way for our community to take part in that promise.

Thousand Kites (2007)

Community members rehearse a staged reading of Thousand Kites, *Lebanon, Virginia, 2007. Photo by Kayla Bensing.*

Production Information

Thousand Kites was written by Donna Porterfield and directed by Dudley Cocke. Original music was composed by Ron Short, Carlton Turner, and Maurice Turner. Script contributors included prisoners, corrections officers, their respective families, and people living in communities where prisons are located. The dramaturg was Dudley Cocke.

The original cast included former prisoners and corrections officers, family members of prisoners and corrections officers, and people living in communities where prisons were located. Original musicians were Ron Short and Maurice Turner.

Thousand Kites premiered in Starkville, Mississippi, in 2007. It was produced and performed nationally by associations of prisoner families, by law-enforcement officials and social workers, by educators and clergy, by teenagers and senior citizens.

Characters and Setting

Guard: adult male.
Prisoner: adult male.
Chorus 1: adult female.
Chorus 2: adult male.
Chorus 3: adult female.
Chorus 4: adult male familiar with spoken word.
Chorus 5: female under age thirty-five familiar with spoken word.
Schedule: adult female with authoritative voice.
DJ: plays recorded music, also may sing and play a musical instrument.

Setting: Downstage right is a guard's platform or a rectangular area delineated by tape on the floor. Downstage left is a prisoner's platform or a rectangular area delineated by tape on the floor. Center stage is the chorus area. Upstage left is the DJ's music station. Offstage is a microphone/PA system, with loud buzzer, through which Schedule makes announcements.

ACT 1

(preshow, DJ plays prerecorded song "Thousand Kites," then "Running 'Round in Circles"; if DJ is a musician, his/her live playing can end the preshow segment)

(buzzer interrupts music)

SCHEDULE I am Prison Schedule. I regulate prison life.

(without acknowledging each other, GUARD *and* PRISONER *rise from opposite sides of auditorium, walk to stage, cross, and take their separate positions facing audience)*

GUARD I am Guard. Not one guard, but many. I have one mouth but speak with many voices. I have two ears, and I have heard many stories.

PRISONER I am Prisoner. Not one prisoner, but many. I have one mouth but speak with many voices. I have two ears, and I have heard many stories.

GUARD I am tall, short, all shades of color . . .

PRISONER male, female, vicious, *(pause)* kind . . .

GUARD & PRISONER *(simultaneously)* don't give a damn.

PRISONER I do time.

GUARD I do time in eight-hour shifts.

PRISONER I do time all the time.

*(*CHORUS *members rise and stand by their seats in the auditorium as they speak)*

CHORUS 1 I am the public.

CHORUS 2 I am the public.

CHORUS 3 I am the public.

CHORUS 4 *(confrontationally)* I am the public.

CHORUS 5 *(intervening)* I am the public.

(CHORUS 5 proceeds to the stage; other CHORUS members follow as they deliver their lines)

CHORUS 1 We are mothers.

CHORUS 2 Fathers.

CHORUS 3 Sisters.

CHORUS 4 Brothers.

CHORUS 5 We are the people who live in communities where fifty new prisons have been built every single year for the past twenty years.

CHORUS 2 You gotta be kidding! You're telling me that in the United States of America fifty new prisons have been built every year for the past twenty years? Who would believe that?

CHORUS 3 It's a fact!

CHORUS 1 We are the victims of crimes.

CHORUS 2 We are the families of guards.

CHORUS 4 We are the families of prisoners.

CHORUS 3 That's right.

CHORUS 2 Not us.

CHORUS 1 We're good Christians—we don't break the law.

CHORUS 2 Nobody in my family ever gone to jail!

CHORUS 3 Hey, wait a minute! My son is in prison, and he's a good man. Not everybody in prison is bad.

CHORUS 2 Not everybody in prison is good! You do the crime, you do the time.

CHORUS 3 Yeah, I used to think that way until my child landed in jail for a little bit of nothing, and all his friends went free as birds!

CHORUS 5 Point: We live in the United States of America, where one out of every one hundred of us has done . . .

CHORUS ALL   *(in unison)* time.

(buzzer)

SCHEDULE   Schedule, Maximum Security State, 2:00 A.M., Pick Up Mail From Buildings

CHORUS 1   *(as mother, moving toward* GUARD*)* I can't say my son was a perfect child, but he grew up to be a good man.

CHORUS 2   *(as father, moving toward* GUARD*)* He was the first one in our family to ever go to college. Said he didn't want to spend his life working in the coal mines, and end up broken-down like his daddy done.

CHORUS 1   No sir, he wanted a state job.

CHORUS 2   He wanted benefits.

CHORUS 1   He wanted to be a park ranger!

CHORUS 2   Well, it turned out there weren't any forest ranger jobs to be had . . .

CHORUS 1   so somebody said, "Why don't you come to work at the new prison. It's a government job."

CHORUS 2   So he went clear to the other end of the state . . .

CHORUS 1   and took the prison training.

GUARD   I started out at one of the older maximum-security state prisons. We had no weapons—just keys. If the keys were taken from you, everything could be lost. My first day on the job I was assigned to let the inmates on the second tier pass through the gate to go eat. The Lead Officer was stationed a floor above me. He was supposed to flip open two cells at a time. Then I was supposed to unlock the tier gate, let the two prisoners pass through, lock the gate back, and wait for him to unlock the next two cells.

   I took my place by the gate as I was instructed, but the Lead Officer flipped the master switch and let all of them, all eighty-eight of them, out of their cells at once. I threw my keys under the locked tier gate, as I'd been trained to do. I was now responsible for getting every single one of the eighty-eight back into their cells. Remember, I had no weapon. There are no words to describe the way I felt. I had never been locked in with eighty-eight men who would just as soon see me dead. But I maintained my post by the gate, and somehow—I don't know how—got them all back in their cells.

When it was all over, I stormed up to the Lead Officer's post and grabbed hold of the rail in front of him to keep from strangling him. I fully intended to kill the son of a bitch. He just laughed and said, "Looks like you didn't wet yourself, or cry like a baby. You might make it here."

(buzzer)

SCHEDULE   3:35 A.M., Prisoner Kitchen Workers In Place

PRISONER   "If you cause any kind of trouble, I'll shoot you." That was my welcome to the supermax from the Corrections Officer as I got off the bus. Then he yanked my eyeglasses from my face and said, "These are dangerous contraband."

I was shackled at the ankles. My hands were cuffed in front of me and chained to my waist with a belly chain. The CO, who was wielding a shotgun, yells, "This ain't church, this ain't school, and it ain't a place to rehabilitate yourself. It's prison."

I knelt on the floor, and a slot in the door about three feet from the ground opened. I was ordered to stick my hands through it, and the cuffs were removed. "Now strip," a voice barked. What he said next, and what I had to do, was so vile, I'll not repeat it. I will tell you what I was thinking: It won't be fun when the rabbit gets the gun. No sir, it won't.

CHORUS 3   *(as mother of prisoner)* When my son was incarcerated, he was in college and I wanted to keep him going. My whole attitude was, though he is in prison, prison does not have to be in him.

CHORUS 4   *(as father of prisoner)* But when he first went to prison, he refused to see us.

CHORUS 3   He felt his life was over.

CHORUS 4   That first year, I didn't think he'd make it. I thought he'd kill himself.

CHORUS 3   We are a close religious family, and we refused, absolutely refused, to give up. We kept coming to visit him, his brothers and aunts and uncles, everybody.

CHORUS 5

A voice for the voiceless
I represent the ones that yearn to be heard
So every word is a testimony
This one is for my homey
Locked up and wondering
How can we fix this system
That got so many locked in prison
Brothers and fathers missin'
Wifeys and mothers kissin'
Pictures of prodigal sons
Praying for their return
Learning to live without 'em
Never forget about 'em
But it's hard when he's nineteen years old
No chance for parole

CHORUS 4

Nothing to lose so it's just another night in the hole
The only way to console the fears of dying here
Is to pray and put pen to paper
Show that he's trying here
To make the most of the worst
Break the curse of this nation
Hooked on incarceration
Twenty-first century plantations
I fly a thousand kites for my homeys
With the hope that this message and these blessings reach
    all my homeys

CHORUS 5

And it's sad that us community fail to see
That we accept the policy

That proves democracy to be hypocrisy
Building cages for babies
Why try to teach them or reach them before mistakes can
    be made
There's way too much money to be made
We all just getting played
While the rich keep getting paid
It's time we examine the reason these laws have been made

CHORUS 4
I fly a thousand kites for my homeys
With the hope that this message and these blessings reach
    all my homeys

CHORUS 5
I fly a thousand kites for my homeys
With the hope that this message and these blessings reach—

(buzzer)

SCHEDULE   5:00 A.M., Insulin Finger Sticks And Shots

CHORUS 2   I raised my kids in a place out in the country, and crime just never played a role in our life. I mean it really didn't. I would leave my keys in the front door so I'd know where they were!

CHORUS 3   Crime? In the city it's hard to tell who's the worst—the gangs or the police. Every day I feel like my babies are being hunted like animals.

CHORUS 1   My baby sister, who I raised, is on the needle. Yesterday I had to go to court with her. Right when we were ready to go up before the judge, she grabs hold of my arm, whispers, "Don't worry, I'm Wonder Woman." Uh-huh, actually said she was Wonder Woman—that nothing could harm her.

CHORUS 2   Then she whispers in my ear, "I just bought two new tires for my Chevy Cavalier. You know, to outrun the police! Don't tell."

CHORUS 1   Well, I've known the judge most all of my life, and I was talking to him and I'm like, "What are we going to do about this situation here? She's crazy! We need to go ahead and get her incarcerated. She can't stop using."

CHORUS 2 "She won't."

CHORUS 1 And he's like, "It's just the system. Can't rush it up. She comes from a good home," blah, blah, blah.

CHORUS 4 Here recently, in the space of a year, I went to two funerals for kids in their twenties. One was a kid who hanged himself in jail, and the other was a drug overdose. And I happened to mention this to a young girl that I know. I said, "When I was your age, I didn't know anybody my age who had died." And she said . . .

CHORUS 5 "I couldn't tell you the number of my friends who are either dead or in jail."

CHORUS 3 Dead or in jail.

CHORUS 1 One's dead.

PRISONER

I wanna be a criminal when I grow up
'cause criminals live good and have all the luck.
I can't have a bike 'cause my mom's too poor
and my dad's been gone since I was three or four.
And what's all the fuss about going to school
when getting A's and B's don't seem too cool?
I'm not feelin' school 'cause I need to get money
plus I know 'bout the streets so I ain't no dummy.
I already been to jail and it wasn't too bad
and after the first few days, Mom wasn't that mad.
I've seen a helluva lot to just be in my teens
so I'm really a man with criminal dreams.
I know the drug game will really pay off
but I gotta get a gun to prove I'm not soft.
Look at all this cash and I don't have a job
and when things get slow I got the gun to rob.
I'm a gangsta now so I will pull the trigger
besides, who cares about another dead figger?

I don't know anything about this legal stuff
and I hate wearing these tight-assed cuffs.
I better take "the plea" 'cause I can't beat the case.
they had too many people identify my face.
Everyone that I call has a block on their phone
but how can that be when I was so well known?
I got a fat old judge and they say he's mean
and I never saw this in my criminal dreams.
I'm in prison now and it's not what I thought
if I wasn't getting high, I would've never got caught.
I gotta hurt the first one who steps out of line
but if I hurt him too bad, I'm gonna run up my time.
The word seems to be "don't go to the hole"
my life sure changed since that first day I stole.
Last year a man got shot for fighting
but it's not really news 'cause nobody's writing.
If I stay up late, I can hear the screams
but I never heard them in my criminal dreams.

(buzzer)

SCHEDULE   5:30 A.M., Pill Call, General Population In Vestibule, Segregation In Pod

CHORUS 4   When they took my son to the jail, he was in a wheelchair because he had just had both of his knees replaced. He was put in a real little room where there were no beds or nothin'. He spent four weeks on the floor. I done okay at the jail, but once I got back to the house and realized that I probably wouldn't live to see him come home . . .

CHORUS 1   They took my baby sister, who was on the needle, from the courtroom up to the jail. Then I tried to find out things, but I could not find out anything. So I went on home. And she called, said there were eight people in her cell with no bed, no pillow. As a child, she always slept with three pillows. So we got back in the car, and went to Walmart and bought her a pillow. I took it out to the jail, but the officer at the desk said . . .

CHORUS 5 "No, we do not allow that."

CHORUS 1 "Just one pillow?"

CHORUS 2 "She never hurt nobody."

(buzzer)

SCHEDULE 6:00 A.M., Breakfast, Segregation Food Cart Delivered, General Population According To Feeding Schedule

CHORUS 4 Prison food—my son says you'll end up with the weirdest stuff being served to you. Not food so much, but, like, condiments. You'll get O'Charley's ketchup, McDonald's napkins. Companies are using it as tax write-offs.

CHORUS 5 I used to eat with the same guys. One of them was originally from Cambodia. We closely inspected our food for hair, bugs, and mud. The Cambodian guy always gave me his milk. I'd tell him, "Why don't you drink it? At least it's something they can't mess with." He says, "How in the world can you drink that stuff? They treat us like animals, and then feed us pet food." I said, "What are you talking about, pet food?" He says, "Look at the carton of milk, man. Right there it says Pet Milk."

PRISONER

> You want to know what my day is like
> Well it starts at five-thirty with that bright-ass light
> Next comes breakfast at six-thirty
> The coffee's cold and the tray is dirty
> First call for showers and rec
> CO already checking my set
> I break sweat
> Nothing new to them shaking my cell down
> Happens all the time
> Still messes with my mind

CHORUS 5

Go out the yard for a break and come back
Now it's time to hit the sack
Wake up an hour later
To some cold cuts for lunch
I think it's turkey bologna
But that's just a hunch

PRISONER

Then I get my read on with the TV on
Gotta see my soaps
Damn! Victor done fired Phyllis
For sleepin' with Nick
Sharon's pissed
But is anyone left that she's not kissed
Then it's read, sleep, eat, stand
Inappropriate behavior with my hand
Hey, it happens
No need for the snappin'

CHORUS 5

Six-thirty mail call
Everyone stands
Many knowin' it's just a mirage

PRISONER

At eleven I catch the news, Jay Leno
A little *Jimmy Kimmel Live!*
Yeah, no lie, I stay up late
but only for *Blind Date*

CHORUS 5

So that's a day in the life of a convicted felon

PRISONER

I've been doin' time eleven years for not tellin'
Enough talk, I got to get some rest
I'll wake up tomorrow same place, same stress

CHORUS 5

Day in, day out, same plight

PRISONER

Same bright-ass light

(buzzer)

SCHEDULE   8:30 A.M., Prisoner Count Standing

GUARD   If you step across the red painted line without permission, it will be considered an act of aggression, and will result in the use of firepower.

PRISONER   All of this was new to me, but you can bet I caught on fast. I guess you could say that prison is a poor man's college, the school of life. You learn about surviving, because at any given time you can be killed.

GUARD   If you approach any person too fast, it will be considered an act of aggression, and will result in the use of firepower.

PRISONER   The officers don't give a damn what happens to you. They're here for eight hours. If an inmate was to be killed in that eight hours, they still get their paycheck and go home to their families.

GUARD   A lot of the inmates, when they come in here, they come from the cities up north. Most of the corrections officers are white, and most of the inmates are Black. It bothers the prisoners, you know. They say, "You're a white person. You're guarding me, and you know it's not right, because I'm Black." They think we're KKK, or something like that.

PRISONER   The first time I let a fellow inmate borrow five dollars, he didn't pay me back. So I went to an Old Head and told him about it. He asked me, did I want to lose the respect I had? So I went to this dude, who had my five dollars, and beat the crap out of him. I did it in front of everybody because I wanted everyone to see I was for real. I was put in the hole for ten days. When I got out of the hole, I was told that the dude that owed me the five dollars had been turn' into a punk. Sure enough, at chow time the new owner of this punk comes up to me and pays me back the five dollars. So that was the end of another lesson learned.

GUARD   Who's weak and who ain't matters in prison.

PRISONER That's what it's all about.

(buzzer)

SCHEDULE 9:00 A.M., Outside Recreation General Population, Rotate Building Commissary

CHORUS 3 When they incarcerate your child, they incarcerate the whole family. Before that happened to me, I never voted. My family never voted. We just stayed home, minded our own business. Now I've wound up at the state capitol, talking to the senators and delegates, and really, I see they're no better than we are. They're climbing a political ladder, trying to look good to the public out here, but they're not concentrating on what's important.

CHORUS 4 The prison only gives my son two rolls of toilet paper and a cake of soap a month! Everything else he has to buy at the prison canteen. We have to send him a hundred dollars a week, because they charge such ridiculous prices.

CHORUS 3 To talk to a loved one in prison, you might as well take out a bank loan. The prison charges us four dollars to hook up each call, and eighty-nine cents a minute.

CHORUS 4 Good Lord, do they think we're millionaires?

(lively, upbeat)

CHORUS 3
> Rogues in the White House
> Thieves in the hall
> They all join hands
> At the Scoundrels' Ball

CHORUS 4
> They dance around
> Day after day
> When it's time to pay the fiddler
> Guess who pays?

CHORUS 1
> Found a big meth lab
> In the house next door
> And Walmart built
> A superstore

CHORUS 2
> Gonna build another "supermax"
> Prison they say
> Ever'things super
> 'Round here today

CHORUS 1, 2, 3, 4 *(in unison)*
> Rogues in the White House
> Thieves in the hall
> They all join hands
> At the Scoundrels' Ball

CHORUS 5
> They dance around
> Day after day
> When it's time to pay the fiddler
> Guess who pays?

(buzzer)

SCHEDULE 11:00 A.M. Lunch, Segregation Food Cart Delivered, Meals Fed In Pods

GUARD You'll get two people with the same offense sentenced in entirely different ways, where one will get two years and one will get eighteen years—no parole.

CHORUS 2 It's all according to what's hot in the judge's jurisdiction.

GUARD If everybody's worried about methamphetamine, then that's who gets the big sentences, bigger than murderers sometimes. When I first started working at the supermax, all the prisoners came here to the mountains from far away, most from the cities. But that's changing, mostly because there's no funding in our community for substance-abuse treatment.

CHORUS 2 It's not popular.

GUARD So they put 'em in prison. The other day a new inmate gave me a strange look, and called me by my full name. Turned out he was a boy I went to school with over on Caney Ridge. I never would have known him—he looked as old as my daddy.

GUARD
> I don't see no faces
> I don't feel no pain
> Population, civilian
> They're all the same

CHORUS 1
> Heard somebody call my name

GUARD
> Black and white
> Rich and poor
> Thief, murderer
> The boy next door

CHORUS 1 & 2
> Heard somebody call my name

CHORUS 5
> Through all this grief, despair, and pain
> I heard somebody call my name

GUARD
> Can't talk to my father
> Can't talk to my wife
> They're living their lives
> While I'm doing life

CHORUS 1 & 2 *(in unison)*
> Heard somebody call my name

GUARD

> I keep having this dream
> And I awake with a shout
> I get to the gate and I can't get out

CHORUS 1 & 2 *(in unison)*

> Heard somebody call my name

CHORUS 5

> Through all this grief, despair, and pain
> I heard somebody call my name

(buzzer)

SCHEDULE   1:30 P.M., Prisoner Count Standing

PRISONER   I work in the library. I'm one of the few who has a job. Most of these guys have to stay in their cells all day, with nothing to do. Every time I'm escorted to the library, they do a strip search. One of the guards obviously has issues. While he's conducting his search, he looks very closely at all the wrong places, and sweats profusely. Sometimes he's eating popcorn . . .

CHORUS 4   like it's dinner and a movie for him.

GUARD   Some prisoners you never hear a peep out of. They're no different from you or me. And there are those who get in trouble most every day. They end up in segregation.

PRISONER   When I was in the hole, the guy in the next cell threw his tray on the officer. I thought to myself, this guy must be crazy! Thirty minutes goes by, then all I could hear was this guy begging the officers not to beat him anymore. I could hear him crying like a little girl. You see, if you do something to one of these officers, they're not going to fight you one-on-one. They are going to come at you ten strong.

GUARD   Adrenaline takes over when there is a dangerous incident with an inmate. But I must keep a cool head, a stone face, never raise my voice, stand my ground, never, ever show fear. Afterward, when I'm filling out the incident report, my hands shake so bad, I have to write it over three times. But I never let anyone know this. Nobody. Not even my wife.

CHORUS 1   (*as mother of* GUARD) Me and my husband, and my son and daughter-in-law, had always been churchgoing people. We were faithful, going to church most every night of the week. But it got to where my son didn't really care that much about going to church.

CHORUS 2   When he came home from work, he spent most of his time on the telephone, talking to the people he worked with at the prison.

CHORUS 1   He pulled away from his wife, his children, from everything—just left us behind.

CHORUS 2   That prison life became his whole life.

GUARD   My brother and me were working minimum-wage jobs until we got on at the prison. Not long after we started, I could see my brother wasn't going to stick with it. He'd say to me . . .

CHORUS 5   "The prisoners hate us."

GUARD   I'd tell him, "They have their own world, and we don't enter into it." And he'd say, "Don't you see how these people live? Young people, old people, different colors, and a lot of them in here for life?"

CHORUS 2   "It's a sad, hopeless place to work."

GUARD   So he quit, and started mowing grass with a push lawn mower and a weed eater out of the back of his car.

CHORUS 1   Says he's a whole lot poorer now but a lot more satisfied.

GUARD   Me, I feel like I'm protecting my family and neighbors, society. I don't ever want to see any of my family the victim of a rape or murder or a child molester. I do whatever it takes to walk away from a prisoner filled with pride and anger who is baiting me. But when this doesn't work, and an attack ensues, I'd rather be tried by twelve than carried by six.

(*buzzer*)

SCHEDULE   Visitation Dress Regulations: "Visitors may wear casual dress that is reasonable and appropriate. The department reserves the right to refuse admittance to inappropriately dressed visitors. The body must be covered. Hems, slits, or splits of dresses, skirts, shorts, etc., may not exceed four inches above mid-knee. Underwear is required. No halter tops, tank tops, or tube tops. No pocketbooks, handbags, or wallets are allowed in the visiting room. Males dressed as females will not be admitted."

GUARD Families, and mamas in particular, they see their kids like they were when they were little. The mamas don't see the things their sons do in here. During visitation, some families come up and rake me over the coals for being mean to their little boys. And then there are others who tell me to beat the crap out of their kid, because last week he talked bad to them on the phone! I'm serious!

CHORUS 3 When we go to see my son, we leave home after I get off work and drive all night. My husband and daughter-in-law, and her two babies, go with us. We get to the prison about six the next morning. They don't open up until eight-thirty, so we sit and wait.

CHORUS 4 If we find out they're in lockdown and there's no visitation that day, we just have to turn around and drive all day to get back home.

CHORUS 3 The first time we went to see our son, we hadn't seen him in five years because it was so far to come, and we had no way to get there. When I finally saw him, I was like, "What's the shackles all about?"

CHORUS 5

> Negativity is engraved
> In the mind of the slave
> Who walks around the prison yard
> Content in his grave
> He don't want to be saved
> Becuz he's afraid of life
> He'd rather hold tight
> While his fam visit the sight
> And drop flowers off
> In the form of currency
> 'Cause currently
> He's lying six under feet

CHORUS 4

> Our fears get fed
> As our tears is shed
> We want to see him alive

But he's here instead
Words get said
In ways that seem kinda scary
Letters are wrote and read
Like obituaries
I miss you, son
I miss you, brother and friend
I hold time that was spent
In good remembrance

CHORUS 5

When he call on the phone
They speak to his ghost
Sometimes Mom's voice crack
'Cause she miss him the most
His kids need him the most
Yeah, they're feeling the pain
They only know Daddy
Becuz they remember his name

CHORUS 4

It's a crying shame
That's why stains be on pillows
And weeping willows
Mourn for his Black widow

CHORUS 5

But he's subzero
And frozen to the fact
That he needs to rise out of this
Inhabitat! And get back
To life! Where good things live

CHORUS 4

In order to get to heaven
Hell is what he gotta give

CHORUS 5
> His bid is
> A far cry from home
> His state number is the
> Tombstone!
> To mark where they buried his
> Bones

CHORUS 4
> Grave

CHORUS 5
> Prison

CHORUS 4
> Yards

(buzzer)

SCHEDULE   3:00 P.M., Insulin Finger Sticks And Shots

CHORUS 1   I never dreamed of a child of mine working in a prison, much less my baby sister being in prison. I just never thought about prison. It was someone else's problem. And now I know to pray for them, each and every one of them, every day.

CHORUS 4   At my son's prison, there's a mentally retarded fellow who's done eight years on fifteen. This man comes from a big family, lots of little brothers and sisters, and they live too far away to ever visit.

CHORUS 3   Each year at Christmastime, we can order little packages from the prison commissary to be given to our son, for a gift, you know. This year, my son calls me and asks if we can send him some extra money for postage. He said that he and a couple other inmates were saving their little packages, and sending them to this retarded fellow's family, because those packages were the only Christmas they'd get.

CHORUS 4   So if that family's whole Christmas is coming from packages that were given to inmates in prison, well you can just imagine . . .

PRISONER

Sparkling coils of razor-tipped ribbon
Atop a metal mesh of fence
Freshly washed by rain
The glint of sun on gray metal
Glistening helix with tiny teeth
It catches my eye for a moment
I am trapped within
My eye can soar to the heavens
My heart is blind to the scene
My mind is struck with a memory
Ribbon of wire with tiny teeth
Carefully designed to cut cloth and flesh
Now catches sparks of sun
A scintillation, a moment's hesitation
Helices bejeweled with diamonds
I seek the treasure in the trap

GUARD

The joy in the despair

PRISONER

The peace of a simple life

GUARD

The beauty that was not intended

PRISONER

But can be seen and kept as a gift

GUARD

A gift

(buzzer)

SCHEDULE   5:30 P.M., Segregation Food Cart Delivered

PRISONER This place ain't about rehabilitation; it's about fear; it's about anger; it's about humiliation; it's about power, who's got it and who ain't.

GUARD It's about staying strong . . .

GUARD & PRISONER *(in unison)* no matter what happens.

(CHORUS *steps forward together)*

CHORUS 4 Don't we . . .

CHORUS 1 the public . . .

CHORUS 5 have a say?

(buzzer)

(PRISONER, GUARD, *and* CHORUS *exit to audience)*

ACT 2

There is no intermission. After the end of act 1, the cast invites the audience to tell their own stories about their experiences with the criminal justice system. This approximately forty-minute discussion is moderated by an individual who ensures that all audience members feel free to tell their stories from their own experiences. Differences of opinion are welcomed, with the instruction that mutual respect for differences must always be shown. With smaller audiences, cast members may facilitate story circles.

ACT 3

In act 3, the moderator asks cast and audience to focus on actions to be taken, based on the analysis flowing from the first two acts. Whenever possible, the evening ends with everyone joining in a song led by the DJ.

——— **END** ———

"Bound for Ameri'ky"

Poetics of Interracial Collaboration in the Puerto Rican–Appalachian Musical *Betsy!*

Maribel L. Alvarez

I. Disruptions

All families have secrets, but not all of them bite into a family's psyche with the same ferocity. Some are little more than harmless anecdotes kept under wraps to save someone from embarrassment, while others are life-altering.

In the 1950s, a portrait of my Afro-descendant great-grandmother became the focal point for a family dispute. My grandmother Margarita, a mixed-race, white-passing rabble-rouser who wrote columns in the local newspaper and spoke publicly about the scourge of racism, decided to dust off an old photograph of her mother and hang it on a prominent wall in the living room. Her daughter, my aunt Bertha, would not have it. She swiftly removed the image of the dark-skinned Black woman (her own grandmother) and confined it to the back of an armoire, where, in her view, it should remain hidden in the hush-hush of the family's history of miscegenation. No sooner had Bertha removed the picture than Margarita proceeded to reinstall it. They went back and forth for weeks and then years, playing in this squabble of pictographic one-upmanship.

In *Betsy!*, a collaborative work between the New York-based Pregones Theater and the Kentucky-based Roadside Theater, first conceived and presented in the Bronx and in Whitesburg, respectively, in 2006 and restaged in Manhattan in 2015 and Whitesburg in 2017, secrets function as a gravitational force that pulls toward the light threads of unspoken connections between generations of racialized immigrants. The normalized history of the United States inevitably includes stories of travel, settlement, and love in mixed company. The facts are generally accepted: The people who came before us, in some cases indigenous to this land and at other times here due to forced or voluntary arrival, engaged in a struggle of belonging and displacement that endures to the present day. In *Betsy!*, however, that familiar story bends in a different direction. *Betsy!* reveals a powerful and often painful secret: The ancestors we claim do not always tell the whole story of who we are.

Like many proud young women of color in the twenty-first century, the protagonist, Betsy García Swindel, is not oblivious to the violence and pain that made her nation and her people who they are. Like many in her Latinx generation, she has learned to use heritage as a weapon of resistance. She has assembled herself "ethnic," neither color-blind nor color-less, but color-full. For all the fuzz about stereotypes, our contemporary Betsy seems grateful that the cultural artifacts passed down from her Afro-Caribbean father (music, language, faith) helped her craft an authentic story of self and artistry. Less discernible, however, is her mother's white legacy. The color mix itself is not the secret, but, rather, the twisted ways in which one genealogy of oppression layers and interlocks with another and then produces a rancorous psychological wound.

In the opening act, we are introduced to Betsy just as she is about to come onstage to sing at a New York club. She is an accomplished Latin jazz singer enjoying a budding career. The announcer describes her as "beyond compare" (*incomparable* in Spanish). Her bilingual, biracial, urban, and sophisticated looks and sensibility underscore her self-assurance. She enters singing a classic Caribbean guaracha, oozing its customary blend of bravado and sexual innuendo. From what we can tell, all seems well in the safe house of kinship Betsy claims as her ancestral birthright. Through fragments of information scattered through the dialogue, the audience is clued in about key events in Betsy's life. Betsy knows her mother and father were an interracial couple who faced rejection on the maternal side of the family, a southern white clan. Ostracized for marrying a Black man of Puerto Rican origin, Betsy's mother, Elizabeth, never looked back at her Appalachian roots, plunging herself instead into the world of Caribbean New York. She becomes the outsider who would make family from scratch. Her love story with the handsome García is ushered sweetly through jazz, a passion they shared, but which in 1950s America was also a "colored" artistic expression that Elizabeth, as a teenage piano prodigy in rural Kentucky, was forced to conceal.

When Betsy is a young child, her mother, Elizabeth, dies suddenly. The child is raised by the father in the Bronx borough of New York, an immersive world of music, dance, language, family, and memories of migration, slavery, tenacity, resistance, and "*sabor*" (racialized enjoyment). Just as her mother succeeded in keeping at bay the pain of family estrangement, so do Betsy's Afro-Latina roots overtake all other parts of her identity. When we meet her at the nightclub, we glimpse a moment of calm before the storm. The first gusts of winds arrive with the news that her father has died.

Family secrets seldom contain just one story. Revelations of one incident often provoke a cascade of other incidents and stories. Some of the most interesting scientific studies about trauma try to explain why things locked away in one corner of the brain can resurface in other areas, the phenomenon we popularly recognize as "triggering." One explanation is that the limbic system stores trauma not as story per se, as in following a syntax of logical sequence, but, rather, as sensory fragments that can supersede the higher reasoning and language structures of the brain through sound, smell, and visual images. We react rather than think. We feel rather than reason. Trauma causes disorganized and disproportionate reactions: A Fourth of July fireworks display can feel like shots fired. When Betsy's father dies, the foundations of her constructed identity as a Black and brown woman in America are shaken. To Betsy's surprise, the ghosts that surface after her loss are not the reassuring ancestors of her paternal lineage—those voices that were soundly celebrated in life through the pride of Puerto Rican, African diaspora, Black vernacular music, and Nuyorican cultural reclamation. Instead, the unfinished business of whiteness rushes in.

As the lights dim, the audience's attention moves from the nightclub scene toward a new figure, Spirit, emerging from the shadows in a dress made up of yellowish papers—the documents, deeds, titles, and proclamations of indentured servants, ancestors who also made an involuntary journey across the Atlantic. Betsy is stricken with a searing pain: Why didn't she know about this other history of indignity? What heinous acts lay buried in the forgotten archives of her family's Appalachian white history? How can she draw a through line from the Scots-Irish womb that gave life to her Afro-mestiza body?

From this reveal forward, the unacknowledged side of Betsy's biracial self will get specific. The first Elizabeth arrived in America from Ireland in 1794. She had been seduced by a sailor, who promised her Atlantic passage and marriage, and when they landed in Philadelphia, he promptly sold her to a tavern keeper. She was fifteen years old and pregnant. To demonstrate her fortitude, she named her bastard child J.C. She was determined to give J.C. the American dream of owning a piece of land, along with her two later children from a tavern relationship with a hunter named Swindel. Elizabeth's daughter, Betsy Swindel (the first Betsy), followed her mother into the tavern trade and west into the mountains, where she fulfilled her mother's dream of owning land—nine acres "on the waters of Elk Creek." Betsy's two sons, Eli and Daniel, joined the infantry on opposite sides of the Civil War, and from there the focus stays on the Swindel women; *Betsy!* is a matrilineal drama right up to the present.

Just at the auspicious time when Betsy embraces the full force of her musical calling, residues of a toxic cocktail of sexual and racial violence in her ancestry demand her attention. The complicated sensuality of being more than one kind of ethnic subject at once will shake Betsy's confidence as much as it will prompt audiences to interrogate what we find simultaneously attractive and repugnant in tales of cross-racial love. After all, *American pluralism represents a kind of reprehensible family secret in its own right*. How we make sense, or not, of the disarray that we are natives and migrants, patriots and traitors, workers or freeloaders, good neighbors or haters, QAnon or "bad hombres" has become the urgent moral calling of our lifetime.

II. Pedagogies

Sitting in the Off-Broadway Puerto Rican Traveling Theater on Forty-seventh Street in 2015 during the premiere of the restaged *Betsy!*, I began to grow impatient at the story. I could sense disorientation enveloping the audience as the characters began to appear. Spanish-English code-switching suddenly gave way to a southern drawl. The syncopated Afro-Latin beat of the opening scene morphed into a bluegrass ballad. *Who is speaking now? Whose story are we following?* I told myself to stay focused and practice good theater audience habits (let the story take you where it must). Eventually, I accepted that the flow of narrative in this musical had not been designed to make the audience comfortable. To teach a grand lesson, the writers of *Betsy!* favor intentionally jagged, nonlinear storytelling. When Betsy is visited by the Spirit, an ageless, shape-shifting narrator who will at times turn into her mother and at other times into the "first Elizabeth," or Elizabeth's daughter the "first Betsy," a difficult pedagogy unfurls. The playwrights offer no apologies; the discomfiting effect is deemed necessary. To tell the kind of turbulent story *Betsy!* wants to tell requires a form of theater-making that is comfortable with ambiguity and equivocation.

Through the heartfelt story of one woman coming to grips with the hybridity in her life history, we are asked to see our own lives contaminated with the fragments of other stories—maybe even some we do not yet know. The dilemma of living with the knowledge of *who we really are* and *what it took to bring us here* leaps back and forth between the characters in the play. The audience has been drafted to be a witness to Betsy's psychological vertigo. The musical score sways from Latin jazz to old-time. The scenic designs rush from urban tenements to mountain hollers. Lights shine bright on Betsy's stunning red dress, then recede in near darkness upon Spirit and her cargo of old covenants. The historical markers (dates, locations, keywords) we are offered through dialogue between Betsy and her ghostly visitors are not nearly enough to help us find our bearings. Watching the story unfold, we sense Betsy has entered the point of no return. Wherever the story leads, it won't let her down easy. But why must her remembering be so painful?

Pregones's artistic director, Rosalba Rolón, calls this unresolved tension "the emotional truth" of the play. It is there to function as a marker of discontinuity, to make the point that we don't know about Betsy as much as we think we do. It is meant to slap the smugness out of our habitual theater-watching satisfaction, what cultural critic Doris Sommer has called that hegemonic "conspiratorial intimacy" by which audiences forgo truly difficult learning and serious dialogue in favor of quick and sentimental "aha!" moments.

Indentured servants like Betsy's ancestors were poor Scottish and Irish men and women who signed a contract, by which they agreed to work for a certain number of years in exchange for transportation to the New World. Once they arrived in the American colonies, mainly Virginia, charges for food, shelter, and clothing were added to their bills. Children were indentured as well as adults. Many met death at the hands of cruel masters or from diseases caused by unsanitary conditions. Promises of land of their own and a place to belong were broken. Poor, uneducated, working white stock—many fled into the mountains. But the racial regime of the time offered a wedge to fight back—some were successful at presenting complaints in court against their masters, and by the end of the 1600s the number of new white indentured servants began to dwindle. The colonial elites soon found a solution. Landowners began replacing indentured servants with African slaves, a more profitable and renewable source of labor.

Betsy's DNA materializes one of the most tragic myths running through American history: For some to be happy, we are made to believe, others must suffer. This belief is the underbelly ideology that justifies extraction, enslavement, impoverishment, and neglect, even as we can't possibly accept culpability. The consequences of this type of zero-sum thinking are dehumanizing. Seldom in our history as a country have we been able to contemplate alternative arrangements. We could have done better, but our imagination for any other way is dry. Native Americans are dispossessed of land in the name of progress and industry, and immigrant children are put in cages in the name of law and order. The suffering of enslaved Blacks becomes naturalized and then forgotten, or, worse, at some level justified. "It is what it is; get over it," conservative radio commentators tell their frightened audiences day after day. It is an endless cycle of blame and disavowal. In the era of Trumpism in American democracy, it is all too easy to assign blame for the failures of our civic aspirations to a pathology of fear, neglect, anti-intellectualism, plain old racism, and a reverse sense of white victimhood. With *Betsy!* the two ensembles saw an opportunity to push past the clichés that tend to freeze minoritized identities into wholesome ornaments. Our collective story, it turns out, is far more complicated than we have had the courage to face.

On popular TV specials about genetic reveals, some of the most affecting moments are when whites, especially those who harbor racist sentiments and views, discover that they have a certain quantum of Black, Indigenous, or brown in their bloodline. The moral lesson is delivered by way of irony: What you hate is also part of who you are. But truth be told, most of us find ways to circle the wagons and avoid the kinds of personal and collective reckoning that would normally be expected if we saw ourselves stripped of the comforts and protection of our respective identities. We have accumulated enough theories about the motivations and deficits of others unlike ourselves to justify anything. Ideologies are like cookies and milk—they feel warm and comforting; they make it all too easy to explain away the ugly, the other, the ambiguous, the defective, the inconsistencies that live within us and next door. Clinging to ideology is a problem of empathy and social ethics. Sadly, we have too many examples indicating that this condition afflicts people at all points on the political spectrum. In *Betsy!* we witness an intellectually honest attempt to puncture this bubble. Betsy's emotional wreck points to a trio of humbling disclosures: (1) we all see what we want to see; (2) we all pick the parts of our stories that best fit the selves we are invested in crafting; (3) we all have reckonings of racial pain in our families and communities that can easily confound our political slogans and well-rehearsed sense of self.

"Can drama play a role in creating a more realistic history of the United States?" asks Dudley Cocke, one of the Appalachian co-creators and directors of the musical. This is a difficult question, not because there is uncertainty about what theater can accomplish as a form of civil rights education (that has been settled in the archives of American history long ago), but because in America forgetting is our religion: forgetting how we *really* came to be, and everything and everyone who had to be broken for us to call ourselves into being. (Gore Vidal often spoke of "the United States of Amnesia.") Were the American story to be told nakedly, unprotected by the sedative coat of national holidays or ethnic pride parades, the shattering of myths might yet prove to be too intense or painful to handle.

But what if we could imagine a painful yet affirming meander around identity boxes and categories? What if we recognized that genealogies confound more than they explain, and racial signifiers are impossible to map with surgical precision? Betsy García has done all of us a great service: She faces these American demons without needing to come to an entirely happy resolution. When the houselights come on and the music stops, we are not entirely sure that Betsy will be able to heal from the racial trauma of her layered ancestry. Pregones and Roadside designed the musical with this refusal of closure in mind. Their creative teams were determined to resist the impulse to suture all the fragments and tie up all the loose ends. Doris Sommer suggests this is the kind of artistic integrity that our times demand. If we hope for serious and useful intercultural and cross-racial dialogue, she says, we must first realize we won't grasp one another's meanings at the first light touch. It we really want art to matter in the world, let alone to transform it, we must insist on making and receiving art that frays at the edges and holds at bay our "aggressive desire to overtake" the irascible complexity of the other in one large gulp of self-congratulatory entitlement.

III. Recognitions

On a crisp Saturday morning in May 2002, I sat in a circle with a group of strangers at a gallery in downtown San Jose, California. We had gathered to discuss a project about Asian-Latino marriages in Silicon Valley, which the arts center where I worked had proposed. Those who turned up were responding voluntarily to a widely publicized call for participants. They represented a variety of somewhat unusual intercultural mixtures: Mexican-Japanese, Guatemalan-Vietnamese, Ecuadorian-Pakistani, and others. As we talked, our conversation began to reveal, awkwardly at first, the nuances of daily life in households where love, or sometimes necessity, had brought distinct cultural identities to live under the same roof. One woman said, "When I get angry at him, the first thing I grab onto are the stereotypes of his culture that I learned growing up." A man responded, "Yes, I do the same, but then I think about our children and realize that I can't burden them with those ideas, because they, too, are part of that culture."

The idea for our Silicon Valley project had emerged from the same familiar impulse common to many community art organizations: to acknowledge untold stories. What we didn't anticipate or prepare for was the less than peaceful collision of feelings that the subject matter of intercultural relationships brought up among participants. They gladly granted permission to have their lives interpreted through visual displays and essays, but rather than "community dialogues," they requested only internal discussions among the participating families. "There are just too many sensitive issues to take into account when you consider the adjustments each one has had to make to sustain these kinds of marriages," one woman said.

I learned a valuable lesson: Intercultural life and work is messier than we think.

Criticism has not always been friendly to the kinds of racial and cultural disidentifications that *Betsy!* advances. For most of the history of American theater, producers and critics have been mostly blind to the complexity of cultural subjectivities. Staging the drama of white power over minority disadvantage has generally had quicker appeal than the nuanced analysis of minority-on-minority dynamics. The musical, especially, says theater scholar Warren Hoffman, has always been "marked by a vague white anxiety about race." Yet race and all its semiotics and undercurrents have always worked their way through the large Broadway hits, in ways both forthright and quiet. Because of its simultaneous flirtations and disengagements with racial politics, Hoffman describes the American musical as a "deceptively potent form."

Betsy! takes a bold leap from generic multiculturality to rickety interculturality. Multiculturalism acknowledges diversity at a distance; interculturalism plunges into intimacy. The multicultural world is settled, needing only the obvious to be pointed out; its public philosophy is civility. Interculturality is transgressive, tangled, and risky; as a political platform, it is aspirational and laborious, and there is no guaranteed positive outcome. *Betsy!* is not satisfied to simply check the box of diversity and level the field of human difference; the musical goes further than illustrating that all racial/ethnic groups love, suffer, and hold regrets with equal intensity. Instead, *Betsy!* does a double take on racial trauma, raising questions about how one racialized experience overlaps another, and vice versa, and how neither contains an absolute truth that can safely protect her from historical anguish. Two questions frequently asked of theater are: *What does the story say?* and *What does the story mean?* In the making of *Betsy!* a third question emerges: *How does the story create plausibility?* For all the risks of thematic perplexity that the production willingly embraces, one aspect of *Betsy!* that stands out with remarkable clarity is the play's success as a collaborative storytelling project. We feel that in the play's abundant humor.

"The way we have negotiated our respective artistic spaces onstage has been as powerful for our individual growth [as theater companies] as for the outcome of the production itself," says Rosalba Rolón, the Bronx-based codirector. When Ron Short, a core member of Roadside Theater for almost four decades, conceived the idea that gave birth to *Betsy!* he was exploring a very personal story about his distant grandmother—the "real" Betsy. "The spark for *Betsy!* was the realization that this was a story that had to be told," he says. "It wasn't a bigheaded idea, but I thought the story had to have value for other people. If it happened here, it probably happened over the hill as well. I knew what the story meant to me, but how do you make that story bigger? The only way is through collaboration. You simply don't know what you don't know."

It was the collaboration that ultimately made the "improbable" story of Betsy come alive. There is no objective statistical record of intermarriage between Appalachians and Puerto Ricans to speak of. There are no traceable lines of scholarship about the intermingling of old-time and Latin jazz in ethnomusicological studies. But the conviviality shared between the two companies over several decades, during which they also learned to share the real estate of "minoritized" artmaking in the United

States, made the "what if" behind the story plausible. Dudley Cocke explains it this way: "Before Roadside and Pregones existed as companies, Appalachia and the Bronx were already playing tag at the bottom of the Fed's annual list of America's most economically distressed communities. After several years of following which community was winning, I reasoned the Bronx must be an enclave of Appalachia's lost cousins—or vice versa. I introduced this idea to Pregones artistic director Rosalba Rolón, and she said we should test such a supposition. And what artist wouldn't want the thrill of working with [other artists] from distinct cultures and different theater traditions?"

When Pregones and Roadside first started collaborating, inventive ways of reading each other's cultural realms began to emerge among the respective communities in each region. Rolón tells the poignant story of Pregones's staff pondering what kind of marketing materials to use for the first visit of Roadside to the Bronx in 1994. "We asked ourselves how to introduce to our Bronx public the idea of an exchange with a theater company from a region that was largely unfamiliar to our community," she said. "Except for the television show *Beverly Hillbillies,* many in our community had no other point of reference about Appalachia." The Bronx team stumbled upon a common geographic element in both Appalachia and the island of Puerto Rico. "Mountains in both areas," said Rolón, "began to spark the interest of the public." Describing the *"Apalachos"* as "people from the mountains" resonated with the nostalgia many Puerto Ricans living in New York felt for the island's central mountain range. Bronxites imagined in their own terms, accurately or not, what "mountain people" would be like and, in doing this, saw parallels where none previously existed. The audience built its own framework for interpretation and empathy.

Similarly, when the play was first staged in Kentucky, some of the Puerto Ricans who had never been to Appalachia found that the hollers reminded them of the casitas that were familiar to them back home in the Bronx and in Puerto Rico. The materiality in these communities' ordinary ways of life became an anchor for empathic recognition, even when outside forces conspired to declare the plights of these two communities sociologically incompatible. *Betsy!* offers a different tracing of the history of marginality than we are used to seeing in mainstream media. Rolón and Cocke believe that nonelite theater audiences deserve more respect than many repertory theater companies are willing to give them. "A popular audience," says Cocke, "is capable of understanding any intellectual argument if it is presented transparently. Through their own story they understand the characters' story—people wrap themselves in content."

Since the play's inception, each *Betsy!* production has generated moving testimonials from audience members about their own family racial entanglements. One man in the Bronx was so deeply affected by the play that he walked out midway through the performance and explained to one of the Pregones team members in the lobby that his own story paralleled Betsy's in ways that he had never been able to confess to his own wife. Yet audience impact work is so much more than emotional stirring. It is also a reckoning and an awakening to types of knowledge that may have been silenced or avoided. In 1994, when Roadside first visited Pregones at their performance space in the Bronx, a member of the public told one of the actors, "I didn't understand anything, but I understood everything." "That line became central to our collaboration in the following years," says Rolón.

Betsy! is not an easy ride for audiences looking for the predictable cultural affirmation that is so much a part of the tradition of community-based theater. As the play continues to reveal the vulnerabilities of past generations, at one point it feels unclear whether Roadside and Pregones are arguing for standing proud in your own identity or for downplaying it as a strategy of survival. Many of Betsy's ancestors navigated these same murky questions: distancing themselves from the hearth, blaming the mother for the injuries of the soul, or, as in the case of Betsy's own mother, keeping silent about the past. "The question is how to build on that simplistic view of identity that we are naturally going to gravitate to," says Short.

"The audience expectation is to see itself in the play," explains Cocke, "but the challenge for us as artists, and with *Betsy!* in particular, was how to make things more complicated. We don't provide a smooth and comfy answer to the dilemma of our hybrid selves. In some ways, the audience knows that our proposal for identity is a crapshoot, but they trust us.

The question is, Am I just an Appalachian in one note or is there more to me and my people?"

If we could successfully condense into a slogan the mainstream American artistic approach to multiculturalism in the last forty years, a good candidate would be "Diversity: Anybody Can Do It!" It is the American birthright to identify a problem and craft a solution. "We got this," declare museums, symphony orchestras, dance and theater companies as they trumpet their efforts to diversify their art offerings. The American artistic apparatus, in both its nonprofit and commercial registers, takes for granted the assumption that art has the ability to represent the stories of others who are *not like us* but from whom we can (and maybe must) learn universal lessons.

The productive collaboration of Roadside and Pregones on *Betsy!* offers something fresh to the mix. *Betsy!* refuses to offer politically soothing ointment. Short sees the play as a triumph of artmaking: being able to go from the "me" to the "we" without preaching about an alleged national soul cleansing that would inevitably be part illusion and part manipulation. "The balance is telling it with passion but not longing," he says. Essentially, the play's nonclosure also doubles as a disclosure: Our national capacity to heal from past shortcomings hinges on a recognition that legacies of pain and hope are both our joy and our shame. As Elizabeth writes to her daughter, Betsy: In the end, we are "never quite whole."

Betsy! (2015)

Performance of Betsy! in New York, New York, 2015. Actors: Caridad de la Luz, Elise Santora, and Pat D. Robinson; musicians: Desmar Guevara, Antonio Guzmán, Jonny Morrow, William Rodríguez, and Sylvia Ryerson. Photo by Marisol Diaz.

Production Information

Betsy! is an original musical play by Pregones Theater and Roadside Theater. The book was written by Ron Short and Dudley Cocke, with Rosalba Rolón and Beegie Adair. Music was written by Ron Short, Beegie Adair, and Desmar Guevara. Lyrics were written by Ron Short, with additional text and lyrics by Caridad de la Luz and Wenceslao Serra Deliz. The play also includes segments of "Olas y arenas," by Sylvia Rexach; "Buche y pluma no más," by Rafael Hernández; and "Majestad Negra," by Luis Palés Matos. The production was directed by Dudley Cocke and Rosalba Rolón. Music codirectors were Beegie Adair and Desmar Guevara.

The original cast included Elise Santora as Spirit, Caridad de la Luz as Betsy, and Pat D. Robinson as Man. The original band was composed of Antonio Guzmán, Desmar Guevara, Sylvia Ryerson, William Rodríguez, and Jonny Morrow.

Betsy! premiered on April 4, 2015, at the Puerto Rican Traveling Theater in New York City and ran for one month. Prior presentations of *Betsy!* as a work in development were coproduced at Pregones Theater in the Bronx in 2006 and 2008. The role of Betsy during the development process was played by Connie Florence and Yaritza Pizarro, the role of Spirit was played by Meredith Burns, and the role of Man was played by Ron Short.

Characters and Setting

Betsy is a Bronx-born singer and performer, the offspring of a Puerto Rican father and a mother of Scots-Irish descent. Spirit is a female able to travel in time and shift shape. Man is a pal of Spirit.

The setting: a Latin jazz club. Lighting and music are used to indicate changing scenes. The band is onstage throughout the play, and includes piano, guitars, bass, drums and percussion, cuatro, banjo, and fiddle.

ACT 1

Scene 1

(show about to begin at Panorama Latin Club in the Bronx; musicians ready, lights down; BETSY *about to go onstage; backup singers help prep her)*

MAN   *(as backup singer; upstage)* Come on, Betsy. We're up!

BETSY   *(offstage)* Pero . . . where's Papi?

MAN   He's not here yet, but we gotta go.

BETSY   *(offstage)* I'm nervous.

SPIRIT   *(as backup singer; offstage)* Girl, do your thing.

BETSY   *(offstage)* My thing?

ANNOUNCER/MUSICIAN   ¡Damas y caballeros! Ladies and gentlemen! Welcome to Pedro García's Panorama Latin Club. ¡Bienvenidas! ¡Bienvenidos! Tonight is Ladies' Night. Es Noche de Damas. Let's hear it for the Panorama Lady herself. The talented, talentosa, remarkable, maravillosa, electrifying BETSY GARCÍA! *(spotlight on* BETSY; *applause, whistles; rumba music)*

*(*BETSY *sings)*

"BUCHIPLUMA NO MÁS"

CHORUS
> Buchipluma no más
> eso eres tú
> Buchipluma no más
> Buchipluma no más
> eso eres tú
> Buchipluma no más

El que ve la lechuza de momento
la quiere matar
pero yo que conozco el elemento
sola vaya pa'lla'!

CHORUS (*backup singers enter dancing*)
Una tarde en el baile lo invite
a que fuera a bailar
Y después que bailamos resultó
Buchipluma no más.

CHORUS

(*suddenly sirens sound and lights chase; single spotlight on* BETSY, *who stands center stage*)

VOICE (*offstage; amplified*) Ms. García, we are sorry for your loss. We tried our best. His heart gave up. Is there anyone else in the family you would like us to call?

BETSY (*slowly, painfully shakes her head no*)

VOICE Your mother perhaps? (*no response*) No?

BETSY (*no response*)

VOICE Arrangements can be made in the morning. We are truly sorry about your father. You should go home now.

BETSY (BETSY *looks up and mouths "Home?"*) After all these years. You and Mom are finally together. In heaven. (BETSY *breaks down; Puerto Rican mountain music is heard far away; it fills the stage little by little;* BETSY *exits slowly; music continues until she reenters center stage.*)

Scene 2

(BETSY *enters the club for the first time in days; she walks slowly; musicians are playing softly; sad atmosphere*)

MAN *(as backup singer; enters and watches* BETSY *for a moment)* Hi, Betsy.

BETSY *(softly)* Hi.

MAN Betsy, why don't you rehearse for a few minutes. It will be good for you.

(she nods; MAN *watches her for a moment, then exits; musicians are frozen; she goes to guitar player, picks up a sheet of music, which she recognizes and hums; she walks over to the bass player, who also is not responsive, and then on to the pianist, who is not responsive)*

(fiddle player enters, enticing BETSY *with a sheet of music;* BETSY *takes it; first sound of thunder—soft; she reads the score and looks back at the fiddle player; second sound of thunder—louder; goes to pianist; third sound of thunder—very loud;* SPIRIT *enters;* BETSY *turns sharply toward* SPIRIT*)*

Scene 3

SPIRIT (OUR LADY OF THE PAPERS—SPIRIT, *appears dressed in long skirt made of historical documents;* BETSY *turns to her, carefully approaches, aware that she is hallucinating;* BETSY *tries to pluck a paper;* SPIRIT *shakes paper skirt and* BETSY *steps back;* SPIRIT *moves slowly, indicating which paper to pick;* BETSY *plucks it and reads)*

BETSY "Dear Betsy, A person cannot die of a broken heart, or I would have died long ago. I love you so much, as the first Elizabeth loved her own Betsy." *(not comprehending; looking at the letter)* First Elizabeth? Her own Betsy?

(fiddle plays "On the Border"; band has become ghostly, playing softly as SPIRIT *shimmers and indicates another paper)*

BETSY *(reaches, plucks the paper, steps away and reads)* "The humour of going to America continues . . . the scarcity of provisions . . . seven ships carrying off one thousand passengers . . ."

(music up)

"ON THE BORDER"

(SPIRIT *sings*)

> There was a time
> On the Border they say
> When mothers sent children
> To their graves.
> The cries of their hunger
> More than they could bear
> In death their wee bodies
> Beyond despair.

(MAN *enters;* BETSY *is drawn to him; she begins to sway*)

(MAN *sings*)

> Our Christian conversion
> Was our blessing and curse.
> They sent us to die
> In the name of the Church.
> Our kind benefactor
> King James had a plan
> To drive all the Catholics
> From Ireland.
> Like a stake we were driven
> Into the heart.
> A wedge to split
> Ireland apart.
> A chance for the future
> Was all we could see
> But the Irish they hated
> The air that we breathed.

(SPIRIT sings)

> But the Irish they hated
> The air that we breathed.

(musical break; SPIRIT gets out of skirt; BETSY and SPIRIT move in unison; MAN sits stage left)

(SPIRIT sings)

> We slaughtered each other
> For one hundred years
> But this land that we fought o'er
> Never was ours.
> No longer Scottish
> Nor Irish it seems
> Scots-Irish they called us
> A dirty breed.

(MAN and BETSY speak the verse as if a prayer as SPIRIT sings it)

> The ships hang like vultures
> 'Round Belfast Quay
> Just waiting to carry
> Our bodies away.
> There's no one to mourn us
> No one to cry.
> It's heaven or hell

(all sing)

> Or Ameri'ky.

(music stops; MAN exits; SPIRIT speaks)

> There was a time
> On the Border they say.

Scene 4

BETSY *(resumes reading)* "By 1794 nearly a quarter of a million Scots-Irish," *(to herself; reflecting)* doscientos cincuenta mil, "had made the journey to North America."

SPIRIT *(singing)* "They say . . ."

BETSY "Most arrived as indentured servants, forced to work for years to pay for their passage."

SPIRIT Some were recruited, others kidnapped, many worked to death, and at least one, your great-great-great-great-grandmother Elizabeth, a fourteen-year-old Irish milkmaid, was seduced.

BETSY I don't know who you are, but are you trying to tell me I'm descended from an Irish milkmaid?! *(music; BETSY's body reacts, moving sensually to the rhythm)* Can an Irish milkmaid do this? *(dances)* I don't think so.

(SPIRIT transforms into the MILKING MAID; music begins; MAN enters)

BETSY *(to herself)* I think I am going crazy.

"THE MILKING MAID"

(MAN sings)

> As I stepped out to walk about
> The streets of Belfast town
> A lovely milkmaid I did spy
> Green eyes and hair of brown.
> I fell in beside her
> Her beauty for to see.

(SPIRIT, as MILKING MAID, sings)

> I am but a poor working girl, kind sir
> Please don't stare so at me.

(MAN *sings*)

> A working girl you may be
> But such beauty is rarely seen.
> Come and sail away with me
> To the shores of Ameri'ky.
> The look she gave me pierced my heart
> Such sadness never seen.

(SPIRIT, *as* MILKING MAID, *sings*)

> How can you speak so cruelly, sir
> To one who can only dream?
> I am a lowly orphan girl
> No money and no means.

(MAN *sings*)

> No matter, says I, for I sail a ship
> Bound for Ameri'ky.
> The milk it flew from her hands
> Her arms they flew 'round me.

(SPIRIT, *as* MILKING MAID, *sings*)

> I vow that I will always be true
> And serve you faithfully.

BETSY *(interjects, speaking and rolling her eyes)* Oh, please . . .

(MAN *sings*)

> I did not tell her a lie
> But I did not speak the truth

For I was charged by my captain
To shanghai or recruit.

(SPIRIT, *as* MILKING MAID, *sings*)

The rich they sail with grants in hand
In relative luxury.
The poor they sail, indentured still
Servants for to be.

(MAN *sings*)

For three long months, in wind and storm
Her comforts I did seek.
And rounder still was her dear form
When we reached Ameri'ky.
I found her service at an inn
Four years her passage paid.
But I vowed that I would soon return
And we'd be wed that day.

(*musical interlude*)

(MAN *speaks*)

And now I am an old man
My crimes will soon be paid.
But there's one sin that damns me still

(*sings*)

My lovely milking maid.

(MAN *exits*)

Scene 5

BETSY   ¡Ay bendito! What happened to her?

SPIRIT   Elizabeth, now a pregnant milking maid, was sold by the sailor into the tavern trade to pay the ship's captain for her passage to America.

BETSY   At least the son of a gun finds the girl a job.

SPIRIT   But there's more you need to know. It was the law in those days that a single white woman with child would be sent to prison if the father of the child would not lend his surname to the newborn, or provide a security bond for the child's care.

BETSY   Obviously there's no surname! The sailor has sailed.

SPIRIT   (SPIRIT *finds a bastardy bond in the pile of papers and hands it to* BETSY) I'm going to make this easy on us. Let's walk! *(music; "Bastardy Bonds")* "A Record of the Bastardy Bonds for the Commonwealth of Pennsylvania in the Year of Our Lord 1795. Child: J.C."

BETSY   "Mother?"

SPIRIT   "Elizabeth."

BETSY   "Father?"

MAN   "Unknown."

BETSY   "Security bond?"

SPIRIT   "Proprietor, Black Swan Inn."

(music plays softly)

BETSY   So the tavern owner puts up the child's security bond, and Elizabeth, now fifteen years old, doesn't go to prison. What does the bar owner get out of it?

SPIRIT   The additional services of Elizabeth.

BETSY   Ayi—the Irish!

SPIRIT   Read on.

BETSY   "Record of the Bastardy Bonds for the Commonwealth of Virginia in the Year of Our Lord 1801." Oh, they moved.

SPIRIT Elizabeth's services have been sold to another tavern owner— this time on the frontier of the Virginia mountains. More walking . . .

BETSY Oh, come on! Again? Those taverns must have been quite popular! *(music punctuates;* BETSY *reacts)*

MAN Real popular!

(music surges)

SPIRIT More walking. "Child: Betsy."

BETSY "Mother?"

SPIRIT "Elizabeth."

BETSY "Surname?"

SPIRIT "Swindel."

BETSY Elizabeth's now a Swindel?

SPIRIT Yep, they're both Swindels!

BETSY "A Record of the Bastardy Bonds for the Commonwealth of Virginia in the Year of Our Lord 1802."

SPIRIT "Child: Wesley."

BETSY "Father?"

SPIRIT "Swindel."

BETSY So Elizabeth raised her three children in the tavern trade.

SPIRIT Oh yes. *(as* ELIZABETH*)* "J.C., stop daydreaming and clear the table. Betsy, fetch the gentleman's ale. Wesley, bring in the firewood."

(music ends)

Scene 6

SPIRIT Betsy Swindel was your great-great-great-grandmother.

BETSY So according to your story, Swindel was my great-great-great-great-grandfather.

SPIRIT Umm . . . want to meet him? *(as* ELIZABETH, *more womanly than the milking maid)* He was a hunter. *(*MAN *enters)*

MAN *(as* SWINDEL*)* Ladies and gentleman, you've all knowed me here for some time! I am James Jimmy John J. Swindel *(*BETSY *points at him;* SPIRIT *nods;* BETSY *reacts)* from the saltworks. Liable and capable of whuppin' anything from a mountain lion down to a rattlesnake. Why sir, I can whup the toenails offen a grizzly bear! I ain't never been whupped but once, and I'm fixin' to tell ye 'bout that.

I went over to Deacon Smith's for a meetin'. When I got there, I was hot enough to melt pure oil. I thought of a pond in Deacon's meadow, went west bent, southbound, in a sort of easterly direction 'til I got there. Pulled off this ol' red flannel huntin' shirt of mine, was in the pond a-bathin', a-latherin' up. Looked out on the land, seen the Devil standin' there. He swore he was the best man that ever stood there. Well, I give him the lie, sir.

He made a dive at me. I stepped back and said, "Now I ain't no man for standin' in another man's way." He took another dive at me. I grabbed him by the seat of the pants, give him six or a half dozen circles 'round that large meadow . . . come to a white oak stump, wrapped his tail 'round that stump and said, "Now Devil, you stand there or you pull that stump out by its roots or your tail, one or the other." I could soon see by the cut of his eye he was gonna stand.

Then I looked and I seen Brendler and six or half a dozen of his hounds comin' cross that meadow after me. I knowed they'd all pile in on me and kill me, or devilish nigh do it, so I said, "Devil, I'm gonna take dexter pass on that rear end of your'n and unloosen ye." I unloosened him. He grabbed me by the seat of the pants, coat collar, pitched me over to the Northside, South of the Mountain, into a beech-gum-chestnut-poplar-white oak tree! Guess what was there when I got there?

BETSY What?

MAN Hornet's nest, peck of stingin' worms or more! Some stung me, some stung Brendler, some stung them hounds. I went on down the road, met that purty little red-dressed Lizzie gal o' mine. *(parades himself across the stage)*

SPIRIT Don't you reckon he's an awful sight?

"DYIN' IF I'M LYIN'"

(MAN *sings*)

> My mammy was a she-wolf
> My Daddy was a bear
> I'm two hunnert pounds tooth and claw
> Covered over with hair.
> Half smoke, half fire
> The other half thunder
> I am what you may call
> The eighth wonder.

> ***CHORUS*** (MAN *sings*)
> > Look out boys, git outta my way
> > Ladies git in line
> > I ain't perfect but I'm close
> > I'm dyin' if I'm lyin'.

> I can whup my weight in wildcats
> I can eat a ton of taters
> Pour enough liquor in my mouth
> To float an alligator.

> ***CHORUS*** (*all sing*)

(MAN *sings*)

> I can set upon a hornet's nest
> Dance upon my head
> Tie a rattlesnake 'round my neck
> Then I go to bed.

> ***CHORUS*** (*all sing and dance*)

(SPIRIT *and* BETSY *sing*)

Look out girls, get outta his way
Don't you get in line
He ain't perfect and he ain't close
We're dyin' if we're lyin'.

(MAN, SPIRIT, *and* BETSY *sing*)

Dyin' if I'm lyin'
Dyin' if I'm lyin'
Dyin' if I'm lyin'.

(SPIRIT *and* BETSY *spin frantically;* MAN *exits;* SPIRIT *and* BETSY *still spinning; stop abruptly as music stops*)

BETSY   Who are these people?!

(ELIZABETH *shifts back to* SPIRIT)

Scene 7

BETSY   Okay. What are you trying to do? Betsy this, Elizabeth that—I am a García. The daughter of Pedro García, granddaughter of Ana María, great-granddaughter of Antonio y Rosalía, great-great-granddaughter of beautiful Coralina, and they were brought by ships as jornaleros to the mountains of Utuado. I am a García. Not a Swindel. None of this other is me. And you . . . him . . . them . . . *y'all* . . . are definitely not my people. As you know. Let's end this madness. Bye! Adiós.

SPIRIT   (SPIRIT *doesn't move*) Ah. You don't care what happened to them?

BETSY   (*long pause*) Okay. What happened? Wait. Don't tell me. He left her.

SPIRIT   Shot into the wilderness right after Wesley was born.

BETSY   Wesley never even met his father. I knew it!

SPIRIT   And Elizabeth rarely spoke of him. When she did, she did so with bitter tears and warnings regarding the reckless and foolish nature of all men!

MAN   *(as tavern owner; hateful drum offstage)* "Elizabeth!" *(drums played as if she is being hit)* "Don't just stand there! Fetch the gentleman's ale!"

*(*SPIRIT* transforms into first* ELIZABETH*)*

"THE CUMBERLAND LAND"

*(*SPIRIT* sings)*

I came to this country an orphan
A refugee from Ireland's green shore.
A woman alone has only two choices
To be a wife or a whore.
I decided that no man would own me
For more than one hour at a time.
I know that many will condemn me
But I claim my life as mine.
My children will never go hungry
I saved my gold and I planned.
Together we will leave this city
And go to the Cumberland land.

CHORUS
Oh, the Cumberland land holds me
Close like a lover's hand
And now I lay me down to rest
In the arms of the Cumberland land.

Now J.C. he is my eldest
He's ashamed of me it is so.
But the others still call me Mama
And I hope that will always be so.
Last night I dreamed of the green hills of Ireland
And I woke with a fever in my head.
J.C. prayed for me most of the day
But I will never rise from this bed.

CHORUS (SPIRIT *and* BETSY *sing*)
Oh the Cumberland land holds me
Close like a lover's hand.
And now I lay me down to rest
In the arms of the Cumberland land.

(SPIRIT *sings*)

And now I lay me down to rest

(SPIRIT *and* BETSY *sing*)

In the arms of the Cumberland land.
And I long to lay me down to rest
In the arms of the Cumberland land.

BETSY   And that was the very first Elizabeth . . . the lovely milking maid. But what happened to her daughter, Betsy?

SPIRIT   (SPIRIT *transforms into her daughter* BETSY) Betsy stayed in the tavern trade. Ah! The tavern trade! The subject of many a missionary sermon.

(MAN, *as* ANGLICAN PRIEST, *enters*)

MAN *(spoken)* "The people of the American frontier are of abandoned morals, and the females are the worst—especially those of the tavern trade. The young women have a most uncommon practice, which I cannot break them of. They draw their shift as tight as possible to the body, and pin it close to show the roundness of their breasts and slender waist, and pulling their petticoats close to their hips to show the fineness of their limbs. They rub themselves and their hair with bear's oil, and tie it up behind in a bunch like a pack of wild Indians. They bear children so young, you will often see a mother looking as young as her daughter, both debauched."

MAN *(as* TAVERN OWNER*)* "Betsy! The gentleman's waiting."

SPIRIT *(to* MAN *as he steps toward her)* That's enough. *(music ends;* MAN *exits)*

Scene 8

BETSY *(eyes fixed on* SPIRIT*)* Betsy? *(*SPIRIT *nods)*

SPIRIT *(as* BETSY*)* Me and my brother Wesley were born on the frontier in the Virginia mountains. They was Indians everywhere then, but that didn't stop Wes. He spent more time in the woods than under roof. When he become a man—he's about sixteen—he took to going farther and farther into the wilderness, *(*MAN *enters, as* WESLEY*)* tryin' to be free, I reckon, 'til finally he couldn't go no further. In 1834, we got a letter from him written from somewheres in the Rocky Mountains.

MAN *(as* WESLEY*)* Again I take up my pen to write you a few lines, which will let you know that I yet survive and am not yet scalped.

"WESLEY'S SONG/I AM ALONE AGAIN"

*(*MAN, *as* WESLEY, *sings)*

For three days the wind's been howlin'
Last night the wolves joined in.
There's frost in the air, autumn is here
And I am alone again.

(musical break)

Today I saw a red-tailed hawk
He was shining on the wind.
He was Lord of all he surveyed
Sometimes I feel like him.

CHORUS

Sometimes I feel like I own these mountains
Sometimes I own the wind
I am the rain I am the sun
And I am alone again.

I trekked thru the Gap after Boone
Into the Ohio country.
Now there's people ever'where
And there's no room for me.
Somewhere deep in my memory
In Erin's green hills I roamed free.
A different place, a different face
But it was the same ol' me.

CHORUS (SPIRIT *and* BETSY *sing*)

*(*MAN *sings)*

Sometimes I think the Lord never meant all this for me.
And sometimes I think that maybe he meant
Everyone should be this freeeee . . .

(spoken)

I dream of a woman with long black hair.
She helped me to be a man
But her and the baby died last year
And I am alone again.

(sung)

> I don't think I'm what you'd call Christian
> But I pray now and then
> 'Cause I've seen the face of all that is holy
> A red-tailed hawk on the wind.

CHORUS (MAN, SPIRIT, *and* BETSY *sing*)

SPIRIT *(as* BETSY; *guitar underscores letter reading)* Dear Brother Wesley, I pray that this letter has finally reached you to tell of the sad news of our mother Elizabeth's passing. I cannot yet imagine how it might find you, since I have no way of guessin' your whereabouts. Brother J.C. says you are probably dead, and don't care no how. But don't pay him no mind. He is takin' it hard. We all know that they had a special bond, which we cannot reckon. *(*MAN *exits; guitar ends; to* BETSY, *now kneeling on the floor, examining the papers on* SPIRIT's *skirt)* I never judged Mother like J.C. did. I couldn't. When my boy Eli was born . . . Eli . . . he was your great-great-grandfather.

BETSY *(hesitantly)* Did you stay long in the tavern trade? I mean, as a barmaid? I mean, was Eli's father unknown?

SPIRIT *(softly)* No. His father was Eli Phipps. He stayed around just long enough for me to bear him another child, Daniel. He never agreed to either of the boys carrying his last name, so I gave them my own—Swindel. But right before Mister Phipps disappeared, he sold me a parcel of land for the sum of eighteen dollars. Nine acres on the waters of Elk Creek.

"MY OWN LAND"

(SPIRIT *sings)*

Tossed and battered
On life's stormy sea
Lies and dreams
Both believed.
Looking back, it's easily seen
What we should have done
Who we might have been.

CHORUS
Today I start my life over
I hold my dreams in my hand
I own my own name now
I own my own land.

I tell myself
No one but me
Will pay the price
For how I've lived.
But when I look in the eyes of my children I see
My whole life staring back at me.

CHORUS (SPIRIT *and* BETSY *sing)*
Today I start my life over
I hold my dreams in my hand
I own my own name now
I own my own land.

Scene 9

SPIRIT *(as* BETSY*)* March 1861. Dear Brother Wesley, I pray that this letter has reached you. I well know I may be addressing a ghost, but in my heart you still live. Much has happened since I last wrote you. My sons have grown to manhood, and though I have done my best by both of them, they have no love for each other. And this talk of war has divided them even further. Daniel talks Union and Eli talks Confederate, but neither talks to each other. Eli says he doesn't need nobody telling him what to do, and that we will all be slaves if the Yankee government has its way.

BETSY Great-great-grandfather Eli está craqueao! Doesn't he know the war talk is about freeing the slaves! And that his own grandmother, who was my great-great-great-great-grandmother, by the way, was practically a slave! He probably owns slaves!

SPIRIT Mountain folk like us were too poor to own slaves.

BETSY ¡Ajá! ¡A otro perro con ese hueso!

SPIRIT *(resumes reading)* As for myself, Wes, I am lost, for my land has been sold to pay for my sons' foolish debts.

(fiddle player plucks a letter from pile; hands it to BETSY*)*

BETSY May 3, 1867.

SPIRIT Dear Brother Wes, I thought you would want to know. As of this date, our brother J.C. has passed away. He is buried on a mountainside under a shade of Cumberland white oak and shagbark hickory. This past year, as I cared for him, I saw his heart soften. *(*MAN *enters and sits downstage center)* In his last days, he started talking with our mother, Elizabeth, in visions seen only by him.

*(*SPIRIT *and* BETSY *move to the portals, creating portraits as "Queen of Galilee" is sung)*

"QUEEN OF GALILEE"

(MAN, *as* J.C., *sings*)

The first time I saw her it was a hot July day
My mother had been bitten by a snake.
I got so scared I tried to run away
But I fell to my knees and I prayed.
When I got back to the house Mother was walking around
She said, "It was enough to give you faith."
She swore it was the tea she drank, so I never said a word
For I knew they would only laugh.

CHORUS

There are angels hovering around us
Visions waiting to be seen.
There are miracles happening every day
Mary Mother, Queen of Galilee.

My mother used to call me Little Jesus Christ
Because me and him was always right.
She lost her faith when she was young
But she never lost her fight
Even until the end of her life.
On the day she died she looked me in the eye
Not one word was said
But she could see the fire burning in my face
And Mary hovering o'er her bed.

CHORUS

I knew my wife before I ever saw her face
Mary showed her to me.
Then one night in church, when I looked into the crowd
Her face was all I could see.
When we lost our first child I nearly lost my mind

I cried, "Oh Lord, how can this be?"
But then I saw my baby in my mother's arms
And they were smiling at me.

CHORUS

(*musical break in which* MAN, SPIRIT, *and* BETSY *dance*)

(MAN *sings*)

Mary came to me last night, said I was going away
How could I never have seen

(MAN, SPIRIT, *and* BETSY)

She has my mother's . . .

(*music stops abruptly*)

BETSY   (*spoken*) How could I have never seen? You have my mother's face.
(*extends her hand to caress* SPIRIT; SPIRIT *quickly exits; lights out*)

——— **INTERMISSION** ———

ACT 2

(SPIRIT *is* BETSY's *mother for entire act*)

Scene 1

(*entr'acte begins with fiddle then cuatro; several times during the entr'acte,*
BETSY *and* SPIRIT *pop their heads onstage from the two portals/exits, looking for each other; when music stops, they both end up onstage*)

BETSY   You are still here!

MUSICIAN   Betsy, are you going to sing?

BETSY   *(to* MUSICIAN*)* ¡Un momento! Don't you see her? *(musicians shake their heads no; then to* SPIRIT*)* See what you've done? Papers, papers, you are choking me with all these papers! It all started with Our Lady of Papers with all these letters on her dress talking about Elizabeths, Betsys, milkmaids, barmaids, hunters, bastards, bastardy bastards, bastardy bastard bonds . . . brothels, whores, Swindels. Women forced to dance in the tavern trade aka the pole! I've seen lots of botherment. Mountains, mountains, all these mountains, not the mountains of Utuado, no, the mountains of Appalachia. War, a Cumberland land, from Ireland to Puerto Rico, all were mountain slaves, slaves, it's all about slavery. *(pointing at fiddle player)* There are spirits in this room, with music, music, all this music. It's the key to set our spirits free. I finally saw your face again, heard your voice again. *(singing softly)* There are angels hovering around us . . . *(to band leader)* Mami's face appeared to me. *(musician responds with melodramatic chord)* Seriously! *(second melodramatic chord; to* SPIRIT/MOTHER*)* You see what you did? They think I'm crazy! ¡Loca! ¡Tostá!

Scene 2

"HONEY COME AND DANCE WITH ME"

*(*SPIRIT *sings)*

>Oh honey, come and dance with me
>I wanna keep you company
>You know you suit me to a tee
>Oh honey, come and dance with me.
>Oh honey, got my two-toned shoes
>Two-steppin' out to the blues

With you I know I just can't lose
So honey, won't you come and dance with me?

CHORUS

Been working hard all day
Saturday night I like to play
Oh babe, we'll make our getaway
And find us a roadhouse band.
Won't it be grand?

Oh honey, dance with me
You know I love you can't you see
Do you wanna spend your life with me
Honey, would you take a chance
On a real romance?
Oh honey
Honey, won't you come and dance?

(BETSY *and* SPIRIT *begin to dance;* BETSY *stops)*

BETSY   I remember that one . . . how you taught me to dance.

SPIRIT   Now let's try a Swindel song!

"NEW GENERATION GUITAR SERVICE STATION BLUES"

(SPIRIT *sings)*

Well let me tell you, sister
When you're riding in your car
You always need to know
Where the service stations are.
It takes a lot of gas and oil
To get you up to speed

And a "full service" station's
Got everything you need.

CHORUS (MAN *enters dancing;* SPIRIT *sings*)
   'Cause we're the new generation
   Carrying a heavy load.
   We keep America's wheels a-hummin'
   Hummin' up and down the road.

(MAN *sings*)

I tip my cap to the workingman
And to the tourist too.
I wave at the truckers
Delivering to you.
The farmer in his pickup
And the ladies out to tea
Keepin' 'em on the road
Is my responsibility!

CHORUS (SPIRIT *and* MAN *sing*)

(MAN *sings*)

So let me tell you, sister
What service is all about.
You'll see me come a-runnin'
When your tire blows out
'Cause I wear this *uniform*
And insignia with pride

(SPIRIT *sings*)

So move on over, baby
And we'll ride, ride, ride!

CHORUS (SPIRIT *and* MAN *sing*)

(SPIRIT, MAN, *and* BETSY *sing*)

> We keep America's wheels a-hummin'
> Hummin' up and down the road.

MAN   I always did like fixin' 'chinery. This world is changing, and some-body's got to lead the way! (MAN *sits on stool stage left*)

SPIRIT   (*to* BETSY) That's J.C., your granddaddy. My daddy. He owned his own service station. Back then, he played guitar.

BETSY   How would I know? I never met him.

Scene 3

SPIRIT   I was only four years old when Father went off to the war. It was 1941. He was in the First Marines. He fought at Guadalcanal. Mama and I moved in with Daddy's mother, my Granny Sallie. Years later, when I asked Granny Sallie about that time, she told me that my daddy came back a different man.

MAN   (*as* J.C.) My little girl barely even knows me now. How can I just pick up and be who I was before the war? That person is gone forever. Why, my little girl can sing, and she can play the piano by ear. She learned it all by herself. It's like she don't even need me no more.

(*pianist plays Chopin*)

SPIRIT   (*speaking over music*) When I told Granny Sallie I wanted to be a musician, she made me a new dress and gave me fifty dollars. Daddy did not like the idea. Mama even less. But Granny Sallie said, "Your dream has been paid for, from the first Elizabeth on down!"

BETSY Yes, it has!

SPIRIT And off to music school I went—in New York City! I fell in love with jazz. You can't help but smile when you hear it. Falling in love with jazz is just exactly like falling in love with a person, except with jazz you never get over it!

("Elizabeth's Suite" moves into Latin jazz, "I Don't Know Yet")

MAN (*as* J.C.; *music stops, interrupting and stunning* BETSY *and* SPIRIT) Elizabeth, you have killed your mother. She has not stopped crying for the past week. How did you possibly think that we could be happy for you? First you take up with a damn nigger-spic and now you tell us you are going to have his baby. How in God's name are we supposed to be "happy for you"? If I could get my hands on that son of a bitch, I'd choke him 'til he turned white, then maybe you wouldn't care so much for him, since you seem determined to do exactly the opposite of what we want you to do. Think about that poor little bastard child that you are fixing to bring into this world. What kind of life could a half-colored child expect? Neither color is going to accept it, and what if it's a girl, what kind of hope can she ever have of getting married except to a colored man?

Think about what you are creating here, even if you won't think about yourself. If you come on home, come on home now, we will help you through this and help you get a good job away from that jazz nonsense and that godforsaken city.

Scene 4

SPIRIT Dear Mom and Dad, A person cannot die of a broken heart, or I would be dead. But I have too much to live for. I have a daughter named Elizabeth . . . we call her Betsy . . . as perfect a child as God can make. I know that nothing in my life can ever quite live up to that moment when I gave birth to her, and brought her into this imperfect world, where we struggle blindly to live up to the perfection of our own creation.

(to BETSY*)* You did meet your granddaddy once, when you were a baby. We took the bus to Tennessee. We only stayed a few hours. That was our thirty-six-hour bus adventure. You didn't cry the whole trip. And I think I cried the whole way back to the Bronx. That bus ride was the last time I tried to make it up with my mother and father. *(*MAN *exits)*

Your dad didn't want me to go because he didn't think that I could bear it if we were rejected. That is when I started to sing his music and my jazz. *(musician nods)* My grief needed form, even to exist. *(pause)* Did he miss me?

BETSY Every day, as far as I could tell. Sometimes he was sad, others angry. He kept saying, "Someday I'll tell you what happened," but he never did. He couldn't take it. He hated everything that had to do with your side of the family. One time the band was invited to play in Tennessee. He refused. "I'm not playing for a bunch of racists." After you . . . well . . . part of us was gone . . . gone forever.

I'm done with this. I loved you. I love you. But don't ask me to love all those bunch of Swindels. Now I know. Your heart did break in the end. Because of them.

SPIRIT They thought so little of themselves, their only balm became to hate others.

BETSY They took you away from me. I was only ten. They are all accomplices. All the J.C.s and Wesley and Eli and that damn Swindel, too. They are all accomplices.

SPIRIT Well, we are all here now. You are a García, and you are a Swindel. *(*SPIRIT *touches* BETSY *for the first time)* You are all of them. And now, they are all you. Come on now, sing for me, sing me one of your daddy's favorites.

Scene 5

"OLAS Y ARENAS" *(by Sylvia Rexach)*

*(*BETSY *sings)*

Soy la arena,
que en la playa está tendida envidiando otras arenas
que le quedan cerca al mar.
Eres tú la inmensa ola
que al venir casi me toca,
pero luego te devuelves
hacia atrás.
Las veces
que te derramas sobre arena
humedecida
ya creyendo que esta vez
me tocarás,
al llegarme tan cerquita
pero luego te recoges
y te pierdes en la inmensidad del mar.
Soy la arena
que la ola nunca toca
y que en la playa tendida
sufre sola su penar.
Eres ola que te envuelves en la bruma
y te disuelves en la espuma
alejándoteme más.

(musical break)

I am the sand that your ocean never reaches
feeling envy of the beaches
ever lonely at their side.
You're the wave that waves
and says good-bye
washed away by moonlight's tide
as I stand alone and cry.

SPIRIT   *(as she sings, she walks into a pool of light, as if performing at the club)*

I am the sand
that is trapped along the shore
feeling jealous of the sand
that is touched by every wave.
It is you the tender water
that comes crashing ever closer
so close before I watch you turn away.

(speaks)   When we would perform with the band, people would line up to hear us! Pedro García Latin Jazz Quintet! Featuring Elizabeth García!

(resumes singing)

Las veces
que te derramas sobre arena
humedecida
ya creyendo que esta vez
me tocarás,
al llegarme tan cerquita
pero luego te recoges
y te pierdes en la inmensidad del mar
Soy la arena
Que la ola nunca toca
Y que en la playa tendida
Sufre sola su penar
Eres ola que te envuelves en la bruma
Y te disuelves en la espuma
Alejándoteme más.

SPIRIT   Oh, I was all García then, but I'm a Swindel, too. So I was never quite whole.

(music continues)

BETSY *(spoken word)*
    I'm the land that is trapped
    feeling envy of the sand
    that is touched by every wave
    as I watch you turn away
    As your wave slowly approaches
    it destroys me as I notice
    that I've lost you and
    I wonder where you are
    It is you the tender ocean
    that comes crashing ever closer
    I wait hoping that you'll land into my arms
    I'm the sand that never reaches
    feeling envy of the beaches
    you're the wave that says good-bye
    taken by the tide
    as I stand alone and cry
    you appear to wipe my eyes
    I know you are the sunshine of my life

(SPIRIT, *as* MOTHER, *picks up paper skirt, leaving behind one piece of paper; goes upstage center, near exit)*

    Now it's tears of laughter
    living happy ever after
    because now I really have you by my side
    You're my angel, my mother, my teacher, my guide
    everything you've shown me fills my heart with pride
    never more will I doubt, never will I hide

(SPIRIT *exits, pulling skirt of papers after her)*

    You're my Mami and I carry you inside.

(music stops; BETSY *turns to see that* MOTHER *is no longer there; she picks up the piece of paper, then her shawl)*

BETSY   If I had a quilt that would make fifty names stand up here, next to my shadow, I would shift the horizon toward the light of my Antilles. If I could free my eyes from the blue pupils that guard them. But I have myself, and my blood is enough. My blood is enough.

SPIRIT   *(voice offstage)* Baby girl, are we good?

BETSY   Yes, we're good. *(she goes upstage center; backup singers prepare her for show, then take places on stage as announcer speaks)*

Scene 6

ANNOUNCER/MUSICIAN   Good evening, Ladies and gentlemen. *Bienvenidos* al Panorama Latin Club. And now, here she is—returning to the stage for the first time as the new owner and proud inheritor of this club's family tradition—the incomparable, the magnificent, Betsy García Swindel!

*(*BETSY *sings)*

> Sometimes I feel like I own these mountains
> Sometimes I own the wind
> I am the rain I am the sun
> And I am alone again.

(backup singers, MAN *and* SPIRIT, *alternate with "Y tu abuela, ¿dónde está?"; Hot Rumbón rhythm; "Y tu abuela, ¿dónde está?" means "And your grandma, where is she?")*

CHORUS

>Y tu abuela, ¿dónde está?
>
>Y tu abuela, ¿dónde está?
>
>Y tu abuela, ¿dónde está?
>
>Y tu abuela, ¿dónde está?

(BETSY *sonea—an improv over the chorus and a counterpoint to the chorus*)

>Mi familia es García de Utuado
>
>y los Swindels de Appalachia,
>
>yo soy de raza mezclada,
>
>mi tatarabuela era esclava.
>
>Y tu abuela, ¿dónde está?
>
>Y tu abuela, ¿dónde está?
>
>Y tu abuela, ¿dónde está?
>
>Y tu abuela, ¿dónde está?
>
>Si vez un espíritu no te espantes
>
>que están aquí pa' ayudarte,
>
>pa que eches pa'lante,
>
>están presente oye mi gente.
>
>Y tu abuela, ¿dónde está?
>
>Y tu abuela, ¿dónde está?
>
>Y tu abuela, ¿dónde está?
>
>Y tu abuela, ¿dónde está?
>
>Y tu abuela, ¿dónde está?

——— **END** ———

Afterword

An Invitation to Populism

Ben Fink

". . . Benjamin?"

I was sitting in the dentist's office, my anguish barely concealed behind a vague smile, when I heard a familiar east Kentucky accent intoning my name. Scarlett had been my hygienist for nearly a year, since *Betsy!* closed in New York and I moved to Letcher County to work with Roadside full-time. She seemed about my age, early thirties, white, with young children. Beyond that, I didn't know much about her.

During my time here, I had developed a shtick: Early on in a first conversation with new people, I would preempt their suspicion of me by cracking a smile and outing myself as a "Communist Jew from the Northeast." Which was not technically true, but "populist Jew from the Northeast" lacks a certain something. In any case, most of the time it worked—first a split-second pause, then they laughed, and then we laughed together. And after that, we could talk about anything.

I'd introduced myself to Scarlett that way at my first appointment last winter, and we'd gotten on fine ever since. But today, two days after the 2016 election, I wasn't sure what to say. Most of my neighbors, of the minority who had voted at all, had voted for Donald Trump. After a year of sitting on porches and sharing stories and making plays and coming to care about one another, I suddenly didn't know if I had a place in the community anymore. I sat down in the dentist's chair, feeling alone and a little scared. Then Scarlett, friendly as ever, asked me how I was.

"Honestly," I said in a near whisper, "I'm feeling pretty awful about the election."

Scarlett did not miss a beat. "I know! He's so racist!"

•   •   •

Nothing about Scarlett's dress or demeanor suggests "activist," "social justice," or "progressive." I doubt she spends much time watching cable news or following who got canceled on social media. She is a Kentuckian, a Christian, a professional, a mom. But she knows a racist when she sees one. And as they say around here, she doesn't care to tell you so.

In the gated communities of artists, activists, academics, and administrators where I was raised and educated, people like Scarlett aren't supposed to exist. From inside our gates, the world appears to be made up of the poor and marginalized and underserved, the victims; the backward and prejudiced and ignorant, the villains; and us, the thought leaders, the talented tenth, the best and the brightest, the saviors. It took me a while to recognize that this melodramatic worldview, once my own, is rooted in condescension, arrogance, and resentment. And I now also see how similar it is to the MAGA mentality, where the good, hardworking people (often, though not always, white) are the victims; the demagogues who claim to speak for them are the saviors; and the invasive minorities and their elitist allies are the villains.

Neither of these mirror-image mind-sets contains any hope for democracy. We can trace them both back to a relatively small but powerful group of wealth hoarders and their allies, who have successfully redistributed most of the resources upward, convinced the politicians and pundits that the resulting scarcity is natural and inevitable, and sold the rest of us on the idea that for some people and groups to matter, others have to matter less. This is the dismal reality I was born into, four months before Reagan won forty-nine states. For many of us alive today, it's the only world we've known.

But it's not Scarlett's world. And I've been lucky enough to meet lots more people like her, in rural Alabama and Wisconsin, in urban Maryland and Minnesota, in suburban New Jersey and Mississippi, in exurban Connecticut and Pennsylvania. They are neither victims nor villains nor saviors, but ordinary people who stand proudly in their communities, their families, their work, and their values. They are young and old, liberal and conservative, devout and agnostic, poor and working-class and middle-class and even upwards into the professional classes, of all races and ethnicities. And given the chance, they will eagerly work with their neighbors across the street and across the country to create a future where there is enough for everyone—a future where the only people who get excluded are those few who seek not to contribute to the commonwealth, but to plunder it.

This is democracy at its truest and fullest: an everyday way of life, where we make our world together and own what we make. For the past century and a half, it's a dream that's been kept alive above all by the populists—not the elite fakers like Trump, who claim to speak for the people, but the homegrown leaders and organizers who make it possible for the people to speak for themselves. Populists have fueled every successful large-scale movement toward democracy in industrial America. A mentor and friend who personally knew Martin Luther King, Jr., once told me "populist" was the only political label he would accept.

Populism is defined by a genuine love and affection for people, all people. This is the spirit in which Roadside calls itself not a theater of protest, but a theater of affirmation—committed to honoring people's innate worth, regardless of the categories or identities they belong to. When people express skepticism toward this commitment, calling it naïve or even wrongheaded, Roadside often points them to the story of C. P. Ellis. Ellis was a janitor and Klan leader in 1960–1970s North Carolina, and in 1971 he grudgingly agreed to collaborate with local African American leader Ann Atwater on a project about racism in the schools, sponsored by the state AFL-CIO. Atwater had every reason to dismiss him offhand, of course. But she didn't. And in the end, as he told Studs Terkel, he became an antiracist labor organizer.

I had some real great ideas about this great nation. (Laughs.) They say to abide by the law, go to church, do right and live for the Lord, and everything'll work out. But it didn't work out. It just kept gettin' worse and worse . . . .

I really began to get bitter. I didn't know who to blame . . . . I had to hate somebody. Hatin' America is hard to do because you can't see it to hate it. You gotta have somethin' to look at to hate. (Laughs.) The natural person for me to hate would be black people, because my father before me was a member of the Klan . . . .

We'd load up our cars and we'd fill up half the council chambers, and the blacks the other half. During these times, I carried weapons to the meetings, outside my belt. We'd go there armed. We would wind up just hollerin' and fussin' at each other. What happened? As a result of our fightin' one another, the city council still had their way. They didn't want to give up control to the blacks nor the Klan. They were usin' us . . . .

When I began to organize, I began to see far deeper. I began to see people again bein' used. Blacks against whites. I say this without any hesitancy: management is vicious. There's two things they want to keep: all the money and all the say-so. They don't want these poor workin' folks to have none of that . . . .

It makes you feel good to go into a plant and butt heads with professional union busters. You see black people and white people join hands to defeat the racist issues they use against people . . . .

I tell people there's a tremendous possibility in this country to stop wars, the battles, the struggles, the fights between people. People say: "That's an impossible dream. You sound like Martin Luther King." An ex-Klansman who sounds like Martin Luther King. (Laughs.) I don't think it's an impossible dream. It's happened in my life. It's happened in other people's lives in America.

The point of all this work, as Ellis ultimately discovered, is to build power. Not power to dominate or control others, but power to co-create with our neighbors and resist those who would divide us and run off with the spoils. One way or another, that's what every Roadside play, residency, coalition, and publication is about: building an ever-growing alliance of ordinary people, rooted in the places they call home, sharing stories and building power and creating community wealth together. Of course, that work is far from finished. It can often feel overwhelming, given the scope and scale of the challenges we face. But that, too, is nothing new.

The populist tradition, which we have seen come to life in these two volumes, offers a place to start. To work in a community, find its centers of power. Look beyond the established institutions and other gatekeepers that inevitably show up first. Keep getting to know more people until you find the organizations *of, by, and for* that community, where everyone is welcome to participate fully. Once you've found them, spend a lot of time with the people there, and get involved with whatever they are doing. (It doesn't much matter what it is, as long as it matters to them. In Letcher County, where we ended up building eastern Kentucky's biggest community solar energy project, we started with square dancing.) Get to know the people, let them get to know you, share stories, and start making things together. Remember that every community has its democratic traditions, even when they look nothing like your own, and your goal is not to change them, but to celebrate and amplify them. And take every opportunity to bring them into work with other communities, including and especially communities they have been taught to hate and fear.

One way or the other, it always works. That's why the exploiters and wealth hoarders pour so many resources into keeping us apart. No matter the external circumstances and the depth of the divides, when people and communities get the chance to share and create together, in a place they know they'll be safe and heard, they will find ways to connect. They will eat and drink and dance and sing and shout and argue. They will create works of inspiring beauty. They will experience the joy and struggle of an expanding world, with unexpected challenges alongside unexpected opportunities and allies. And they will recognize that together we can make tomorrow look different from yesterday.

This is the simple and world-shaking promise of populism—begun by the Farmers Alliances and People's Party of the 1880s and 1890s, which organized the first major opposition to corporate control over ordinary people's lives; passed down through their close collaborators in the United Mine Workers of America, which formed the core of the Congress of Industrial Organizations (CIO) that led the 1930s labor movement and lifted millions out of poverty; and carried by these labor leaders into the civil rights movement.

From there it's a direct line to Roadside, to me, and to you.

Bibliography

Alinsky, Saul D. 1946. *Reveille for Radicals.* Chicago: University of Chicago Press.

Alvarez, Maribel. 2005. "There's Nothing Informal About It: Participatory Arts Within the Cultural Ecology of Silicon Valley," *GIA Reader* 16, 3. https://giarts.org/article/theres-nothing-informal-about-it.

Atlas, Caron. 2011. *Bridge Conversations: People Who Live and Work in Multiple Worlds.* New York: Arts & Democracy.

Auden, W. H., ed. (1939) 1979. *The Oxford Book of Light Verse.* New York: Oxford University Press.

Bedoya, Roberto. 2004. "U.S. Cultural Policy: Its Politics of Participation, Its Creative Potential." National Performance Network. https://npnweb.org/wp-content/content/files/CulturalPolicy.pdf.

Berry, Wendell. 2001. *Jayber Crow.* Berkeley, CA: Counterpoint

———. 2012. *A Continuous Harmony: Essays Cultural and Agricultural.* Berkeley, CA: Counterpoint.

Boal, Augusto. 1979. *Theatre of the Oppressed.* Translated by Charles A. McBride & Maria Odilia Leal McBride. New York: Theatre Communications Group.

Borrup, Tom. 2006. *The Creative Community Builder's Handbook: How to Transform Communities Using Local Assets, Arts, and Culture.* St. Paul, MN: Fieldstone Alliance.

Borwick, Doug, ed. 2012. *Building Communities, Not Audiences: The Future of the Arts in the United States.* Winston-Salem, NC: Arts Engaged.

Boyte, Harry C. 1981. "Populism and the Left." *democracy* 1, 2:53–66. https://academia.edu/15103581/Populism_and_the_left_The_alternative_citizen_politics.

Branscome, Jim. 1971. *Annihilating the Hillbilly: The Appalachians' Struggle with America's Institutions.* Huntington, WV: Appalachian Movement Press.

Brueggemann, Walter. (1978) 2001. *The Prophetic Imagination*, 2d ed. Minneapolis: Fortress Press.

Carawan, Guy and Candie Carawan. 1996. *Voices from the Mountains: The People of Appalachia—Their Faces, Their Words, Their Songs.* Athens: University of Georgia Press.

Carson, Jo. (1989) 1991. *Stories I Ain't Told Nobody Yet: Selections from the People Pieces.* New York: Theatre Communications Group.

Cleveland, William. 2008. *Art and Upheaval: Artists on the World's Frontlines.* Oakland, CA: New Village Press.

Cocke, Dudley. 2004. "Art in a Democracy." *TDR: The Drama Review* 48, 3 (T183): 165–73. https://doi.org/10.1162/1054204041667677.

———. 2015. "Community Cultural Development as a Site of Joy, Struggle, and Transformation." In *Arts and Community Change: Exploring Cultural Development Policies, Practices, and Dilemmas,* edited by Max O. Stephenson, Jr., and A. Scott Tate, 136–65. London: Routledge. https://roadside.org/asset/community-cultural-development-site-joy-struggle-and-transformation.

———. 2016. "The Unreported Arts Recession of 1997." Roadside.org. February 5. roadside.org/asset/unreported-arts-recession-1997.

———. 2018. "Roots, Routes, Alternate." Alternate ROOTS. April 25. https://alternateroots.org/roots-routes-alternate.

Cocke, Dudley, Craig McGarvey, Erica Kohl, Linda Frye Burnham, and James Quay. 2015. "Booklet: Connecting Californians—An

Inquiry into the Role of Story in Strengthening Communities."
Roadside.org. September 14. https://roadside.org/asset/booklet-
connecting-californians-inquiry-role-story-strengthening-
communities.

Cocke, Dudley, Harry Newman, and Janet Salmons-Rue, eds. 1993.
*From the Ground Up: Grassroots Theater in Historical and
Contemporary Perspective.* Ithaca, NY: Cornell University Press.

Cocke, Dudley, Donna Porterfield, and Edward Wemytewa, eds. 2002.
Journeys Home: Revealing a Zuni-Appalachia Collaboration. Zuni,
NM: Zuni A:shiwi Publishing.

Cohen-Cruz, Jan. 1995. "The American Festival Project." In *But Is It
Art?* edited by Nina Felshin, 119–40. Seattle: Bay Press.

———. 2005. *Local Acts: Community-Based Performance in the United
States.* New Brunswick, NJ: Rutgers University Press.

———. 2010. *Engaging Performance: Theatre as Call and Response.*
New York: Routledge.

Davis, Dee. 2021. "Q&A: Author Gurney Norman in Conversation
with Daily Yonder Publisher, Dee Davis." *Daily Yonder.* August 9.
dailyyonder.com/author-gurney-norman-in-conversation-with-dee-
davis/2021/08/09.

deNobriga, Kathie, and Valetta Anderson, eds. 1994. *Alternate ROOTS:
Plays from the Southern Theater.* Portsmouth, NH: Heinemann.

Dent, Thomas, Richard Schechner, and Gilbert Moses, eds. 1969.
*The Free Southern Theater by the Free Southern Theater: A
Documentary of the South's Radical Black Theater, with Journals,
Letters, Poetry, Essays and a Play Written by Those Who Built It.*
New York: Bobbs-Merrill.

de Tocqueville, Alexis. (1835–1840) 1969. *Democracy in America.*
Translated by George Lawrence. Edited by J.P. Mayer. New York:
Anchor Books/Doubleday.

Dixon, Don, Bland Simpson, and Jim Wann. 2006. *King Mackerel &
The Blues Are Running*

———. (Album). Englewood, NJ: Sugar Hill. https://www.youtube.
com/watch?v=zcrWm9s_Cjk&list=RDzcrWm9s_Cjk&index=1.

Earley, Tony. 2008. *The Blue Star.* New York: Back Bay Books.

Eller, Ron. 1982. *Miners, Millhands, and Mountaineers: Industrialization of the Appalachian South, 1880–1930*. Knoxville: University of Tennessee Press.

Erdrich, Louise. 2020. *The Night Watchman*. New York: HarperCollins.

Evans, Sara M., and Harry C. Boyte. (1986) 1992. *Free Spaces: The Sources of Democratic Change in America*. Chicago: University of Chicago Press.

Fesette, Nicholas, Bruce Levitt, and Jayme Kilburn. 2021. "Prison Theatre and the Right to Look." *Research in Drama Education: The Journal of Applied Theatre and Performance* 26, 3: 461–76. https://tandfonline.com/doi/abs/10.1080/13569783.2021.1938989.

Fink, Ben. 2015. "Constructing a Bridge Culture." *HowlRound,* March 23. https://howlround.com/constructing-bridge-culture.

———. 2017. "Building Democracy in 'Trump Country.'" Billmoyers. com. March 10. https://billmoyers.com/story/thursday-building-democracy-trump-country/.

———. 2020. "Secular Communion in the Coalfields: The Populist Aesthetic and Practice of Roadside Theater." *TDR: The Drama Review* 64, 4 (T248): 16–43. https:// roadside.org/asset/secular-communion-coalfields-populist-aesthetic-and-practice-roadside-theater.

Fink, Ben, and Denise Griffin Johnson. 2020. "On Cultural Organizing and Performing Our Future." *Americans for the Arts.* April 21, https://blog.americansforthearts.org/2020/04/21/on-cultural-organizing-and-performing-our-future.

Flanagan, Hallie. (1940) 1985. *Arena*. New York: Limelight Editions.

Fluharty, Matthew. 2013. "Nothing's Free in This Country, And There's No Place to Hide: Listening to the American Bottom." *The American Bottom*. https://theamericanbottom.org/itinerary Four.html.

Forster, E. M. (1927) 2005. *Aspects of the Novel*. New York: Penguin.

Frank, Thomas. 2020. *The People, No: A Brief History of Anti-Populism*. New York: Metropolitan Books.

Freire, Paulo. 1970. *Pedagogy of the Oppressed*. Translated by Myra Bergman Ramos. New York: Seabury.

Gard, Robert. 1955. *Grassroots Theater: A Search for Regional Arts in America.* Madison: University of Wisconsin Press.

Gard, Robert, and Gertrude S. Burley. 1959. *Community Theatre: Idea and Achievement.* New York: Duell, Sloan and Pearce.

Gaventa, John. 1982. *Power and Powerlessness: Quiescence and Rebellion in an Appalachian Valley.* Champaign: University of Illinois Press.

Goldbard, Arlene. 2006. *New Creative Community: The Art of Cultural Development.* Oakland, CA: New Village Press.

Goodwyn, Lawrence. 1978. *The Populist Moment: A Short History of the Agrarian Revolt in America.* New York: Oxford University Press.

Haft, Jamie. 2015. "Becoming a Civic Artist." In *Democracy's Education: Public Work, Citizenship, and the Future of Colleges and Universities,* edited by Harry C. Boyte, 141–46. Nashville, TN: Vanderbilt University Press.

———. 2018. "Creating a Populist Theatre." In *Theatre, Performance and Change,* edited by Stephani Etheridge Woodson and Tamara Underiner, 111–21. London: Palgrave Macmillan.

Handwerker, Margo, ed. 2014. *A Decade of Country Hits: Art on the Rural Frontier.* Prinsenbeek, Netherlands: Jap Sam.

Hoffman, Warren. 2020. *The Great White Way: Race and the Broadway Musical.* New Brunswick, NJ: Rutgers University Press.

Holden, John. 2006. *Cultural Value and the Crisis of Legitimacy: Why Culture Needs a Democratic Mandate.* London: Demos.

Horton, Myles, with Herbert Kohl and Judy Kohl. 1998. *The Long Haul: An Autobiography.* New York: Teachers College, Columbia University.

Hurston, Zora Neale. 2001. *Every Tongue Got to Confess: Negro Folktales from the Gulf States.* New York: HarperCollins.

Hutchinson, Gladstone Fluney, and Dudley Cocke. 2014. "Podcast: A Conservative Economist on Cultural Development." https://soundcloud.com/roadside-theater/podcast-economic-and-cultural.

Jones, Alex S. 2009. *Losing the News: The Future of the News That Feeds Democracy.* New York: Oxford University Press.

King, Martin Luther, Jr.1986. *A Testament of Hope: The Essential Writings and Speeches.* Edited by James Melvin Washington. New York: HarperCollins.

Knight, Keith, Mat Schwarzman, et al. 2006. *Beginner's Guide to Community-Based Arts.* Oakland, CA: New Village Press.

Korza, Pam, Barbara Schaffer Bacon, and Andrea Assaf. 2005. *Civic Dialogue, Arts & Culture: Findings from Animating Democracy.* Washington, DC: Americans for the Arts.

Leonard, Robert H., and Ann Kilkelly. 2006. *Performing Communities: Grassroots Ensemble Theaters Deeply Rooted in Eight U.S. Communities.* Oakland, CA: New Village Press.

Lerman, Liz. 2014. *Hiking the Horizontal: Field Notes from a Choreographer.* Middletown, CT: Wesleyan University Press.

Lerner, Ruby, and Alice Garrard. 2007. "Ruby Lerner, Executive Director, Creative Capital." *Philanthropy News Digest.* October 8. https://philanthropynewsdigest.org/newsmakers/ruby-lerner-executive-director-creative-capital.

Lewis, Ferdinand, ed. 2005. *Ensemble Works: An Anthology.* New York: Theatre Communications Group.

Lewis, Helen Matthews, ed. 1978. *Colonialism in Modern America: The Appalachian Case.* Boone, NC: Appalachian Consortium.

———. 2012. *Living Social Justice in Appalachia,* edited by Patricia D. Beaver and Judith Jennings. Lexington: University Press of Kentucky.

Lomax, Alan. (1972) 1985. "An Appeal for Cultural Equity." In *Program of the Festival of American Folklife,* edited by Thomas Vennum, Jr. Washington, DC: Smithsonian Institution. http://culturalequity.org/alan-lomax/appeal.

London, Todd. 2013. *An Ideal Theater: Founding Visions for a New American Art.* New York: Theatre Communications Group.

López, Arnaldo. 2000. "Fire & Promise: A Saga of Collaboration." *American Theatre.* March. http://roadside.org/asset/article-fire-promise-saga-collaboration.

McClay, Wilfred M. 2019. *Land of Hope: An Invitation to the Great American Story.* New York: Encounter Books.

MacLean, Nancy. 2017. *Democracy in Chains: The Deep History of the Radical Right's Stealth Plan for America.* New York: Viking.

McWhorter, Diane. 2001. *Carry Me Home: Birmingham, Alabama: The Climactic Battle of the Civil Rights Revolution.* New York: Simon & Schuster.

Martin, Randy, ed. 2015. *The Routledge Companion to Art and Politics.* New York: Routledge.

Morrison, Toni. 2008. *A Mercy.* New York: Alfred A. Knopf.

Mullins Family, and Roadside Theater. 2002. *Wings to Fly* (Album). Roanoke, VA: Copper Creek. https://soundcloud.com/roadside-theater/sets/wings-to-fly-songs.

Norman, Gurney. 1977. *Kinfolks: The Wilgus Stories.* Frankfort, KY: Gnomon Press.

O'Neal, John. 1968. "Motion of the Ocean." *TDR: The Drama Review* 12, 4: 70–77. https://jstor.org/stable/i247894.

———. 1999. "A Road Through the Wilderness." In *A Sourcebook of African-American Performance*, edited by Annemarie Bean, 97–101. London: Routledge.

———. 2016. *Don't Start Me to Talking: Plays of Struggle and Liberation.* New York: Theatre Communications Group.

Payne, Charles M. 1995. *I've Got the Light of Freedom: The Organizing Tradition and the Mississippi Freedom Struggle.* Berkeley: University of California Press.

Pennekamp, Peter H., with Anne Focke. 2013. "Philanthropy and the Regeneration of Community Democracy." Kettering Foundation. https://kettering.org/catalog/product/philanthropy-and-regeneration-community-democracy.

Pollack, Norman, ed. 1967. *The Populist Mind.* New York: Bobbs-Merrill.

Porterfield, Donna. 1998. "Appalachia's Roadside Theater: Celebration of a Community's Culture." In *The Citizen Artist: 20 Years of Art in the Public Arena,* edited by Linda Frye Burnham and Steven Durland, 201–206. Gardiner, NY: Critical Press.

———. 2018. "A Theater of Affirmation." Roadside.org. March 14. https://roadside.org/news/theater-affirmation.

Putnam, Robert D. 2001. *Bowling Alone: The Collapse and Revival of American Community.* New York: Touchstone Books.

Rauch, Bill. 2012. "Company: Keynote Speech from the Thirty-Second Mid-America Theatre Conference." *Theatre History Studies* 32 (2012): 1–15. https://muse.jhu.edu/article/520585.

Roberts, Leonard W. (1955) 1988. *South from Hell-fer-Sartin: Kentucky Mountain Folk Tales.* Lexington: University Press of Kentucky.

Rohd, Michael. 1998. *Theatre for Community, Conflict & Dialogue: The Hope Is Vital Training Manual.* Portsmouth, NH: Heinemann.

Rustin, Bayard. 1965. "From Protest to Politics: The Future of the Civil Rights Movement." *Commentary.* February. https://commentary. org/articles/bayard-rustin-2/from-protest-to-politics-the-future-of-the-civil-rights-movement.

———. 1971. "The Blacks and the Unions." *Harpers.* May. https:// harpers.org/archive/1971/05/the-blacks-and-the-unions.

———. 2003. *Time on Two Crosses: The Collected Writings of Bayard Rustin.* Edited by Devon W. Carbado and Donald Weise. Jersey City, NJ: Cleis Press.

Saunders, Frances Stonor. 2001. *The Cultural Cold War: The CIA and the World of Arts and Letters.* New York: The New Press.

Schechner, Richard. 1985. *Between Theater and Anthropology.* Philadelphia: University of Pennsylvania Press.

Sen, Amartya. 1999. *Development as Freedom.* New York: Alfred A. Knopf.

Sharp, Cecil. (1932) 2012. *English Folk Songs from the Southern Appalachians.* Vols 1 and 2. Northfield, MN: Loomis House Press.

Shelby, Anne. 2007. *The Adventures of Molly Whuppie and Other Appalachian Folktales.* Chapel Hill: University of North Carolina Press.

Sidford, Holly. 2011. "Fusing Arts, Culture and Social Change." *National Committee for Responsible Philanthropy.* October 23. https://ncrp.org/publication/fusing-arts-culture-social-change.

Sidford, Holly, and Alexis Frasz. 2017. "Not Just Money: Where Is the Money Going?" Helicon Collaborative. https://heliconcollab.net/ our_work/not-just-money.

Smith, Lee. 1988. *Fair and Tender Ladies.* New York: Ballantine Books.

Sommer, Doris. 1999. *Proceed with Caution, When Engaged by Minority Writing in the Americas.* Cambridge, MA: Harvard University Press.

Spellman, A. B. 2008. *Things I Must Have Known.* Minneapolis: Coffee House Press.

"Student Nonviolent Coordinating Committee Founding Statement." 1960. Civil Rights Movement Archive. April 15–17. https://crmvet. org/docs/sncc1.htm.

Szuberla, Nick. Working Narratives.

workingnarratives.org.

Tchen, John Kuo Wei, and Dylan Yeats, eds. 2014. *Yellow Peril!: An Archive of Anti-Asian Fear.* New York: Verso.

Terkel, Studs. 1980. "C. P. Ellis." In *American Dreams: Lost and Found,* 200–212. New York: Pantheon Books.

Thandeka. (1999) 2006. *Learning to Be White: Money, Race, and God in America.* New York: Continuum.

Thiong'o, Ngũgĩ wa. 1986. *Decolonising the Mind: The Politics of Language in African Literature.* Portsmouth, NH: Heinemann.

———. 1997. "Enactments of Power: The Politics of Performance Space." *TDR: The Drama Review* 41, 4: 11–30. https://doi. org/10.2307/1146606.

Thompson, James. 2012. *Applied Theatre: Bewilderment and Beyond.* New York: Oxford University Press.

United Nations. 1948. The Universal Declaration of Human Rights. https://un.org/en/about-us/universal-declaration-of-human-rights.

Unsworth, Barry. 1996. *Morality Play.* New York: Norton.

Valdez, Luis. 1992. *Zoot Suit and Other Plays.* Houston: Arte Publico Press.

Valdez, Mark. 2007. "Report: *Thousand Kites* Project." Roadside.org. March. https://roadside.org/asset/report-thousand-kites-project.

Vega, Marta Moreno, and Cheryll Y. Greene, eds. 1993. *Voices from the Battlefront: Achieving Cultural Equity.* Trenton, NJ: Africa World Press.

Wright, Charles. 1998. *Black Zodiac: Poems.* New York: Farrar, Straus and Giroux.

Index

About the Contributors

Maribel Alvarez, Ph.D., is an anthropologist, folklorist, writer, and curator. She holds the Jim Griffith Chair in Public Folklore at the Southwest Center, University of Arizona, and is the founder of the Southwest Folklife Alliance. In 2018, the American Folklore Society awarded her the prestigious Americo Paredes Prize for "excellence in integrating scholarship and engagement with the people and communities one studies."

Dudley Cocke was director of Roadside Theater from 1978 to 2018, and from 2012 to 2014 he simultaneously served as acting director of the Appalachian arts and humanities center Appalshop, of which Roadside is one part. Under his direction, the ensemble performed and conducted residencies in forty-eight states, with extended runs Off-Broadway, and represented the United States at international festivals across Europe. In addition to his primary responsibilities at Roadside, which included stage directing and playwriting, he was involved in a full range of nonprofit arts activity: His essays on arts and culture policy have been published nationally and internationally, he cofounded two national multicultural arts coalitions, he served on the boards of three private philanthropic foundations, and he was regularly tapped to advise the National Endowments for the Arts and Humanities. In 2002, he received the Heinz Award for Arts and Humanities. He is an editor of this anthology.

Ben Fink worked with the Roadside ensemble from 2015 through 2020, as a member of the *Betsy!* Scholars' Circle, as the founding organizer of the Letcher County Culture Hub and the Performing Our Future coalition, and as the cofounder of the cross-partisan dialogue project Hands Across the Hills. He has also served as dramaturg on the German premieres of two Broadway musicals, made theater with Turkish and Arab high school students, and chaired a Lutheran faith community in Minnesota. His work in theater, organizing, pedagogy, and economic development has been featured by Salon.com, the Brookings Institution, *TDR/The Drama Review,* Harvard Law School, Americans for the Arts, PolicyLink, and the National Endowment for the Arts. In 2020, Ben was recognized by *Time* magazine as one of "27 People Bridging Divides Across America." He is the general editor of this anthology.

Arnaldo J. López is a cultural worker with a Ph.D. in Latin/o American Literatures and Cultures from New York University. He first joined Pregones Theater when the company set out to transform a South Bronx warehouse into a vibrant performing arts center, and later helped engineer a merger with the historic Puerto Rican Traveling Theater in Manhattan. Versed in a broad set of creative, community, and nonprofit topics, he works with artists in mapping paths toward joyful and sustainable practice. His background also includes ten years in letterpress and graphic design.

The Reverend Preston Mitchell is a retired educator who served as a deacon in the Episcopal Church from 2013 to 2020. He remains involved with the Rideshare program, which was suspended during the pandemic but anticipates returning to serve the families of people incarcerated in southwest Virginia prisons.

Donna Porterfield was managing director of Roadside Theater from 1979 to 2019, with oversight responsibility for all of the theater's personnel and financial matters. She was elected to six terms as chair of the Appalshop board of directors. Her playwriting credits include *Thousand Kites, Voices from the Battlefront, Junebug/Jack,* and *Corn Mountain/Pine Mountain:*

Following the Seasons. She conducted dozens of cultural development residencies in communities across the country and served as a policy adviser for federal and state arts agencies. Born in Berkeley County, West Virginia on a small family farm, she grew up surrounded by extended family, music, and storytelling, until her family moved to northern Virginia for work. Before joining Roadside, she was a respiratory therapist and a first-grade teacher. Since her retirement, she has remained active in her church and her Norton, Virginia, community. She is an editor of this anthology.

Ron Short joined Roadside Theater in 1979 and worked as a playwright, composer, musician, and performer until his retirement in 2014. As the ensemble's leading playwright, he wrote and performed in more than a dozen main-stage Roadside plays, all of which toured nationally. There have been two major recordings of his music, and his original composition for orchestra premiered at the University of Virginia at Wise, his alma mater. He was the ensemble's lighting designer and conducted scores of multiyear artistic residencies in communities and universities. He was raised on a hillside farm in Dickenson County, Virginia, and has carried on his family's gospel singing tradition, which dates back to the 1800s. He lives on the side of a mountain in Duffield, Virginia, with his wife, Joan Boyd Short, and he plays in his "hobby band," Ron Short and the Possum Playboys. He is an editor of this anthology.

A. B. Spellman is a poet and essayist. He has written extensively on jazz. For thirty years he worked at the National Endowment for the Arts; for about half that time, he was director of the Expansion Arts Program, and the other half he was deputy chairman.